ABRAHAM LINCOLN'S
INTELLECTUAL
DEVELOPMENT

1809-1837

To: Ann & Bob
Dear friends
and relatives

Vito Silvestri
Dec. 30, 2013

Vito N. Silvestri, Ph.D.
and Alfred P. Lairo

Wasteland Press

www.wastelandpress.net
Shelbyville, KY USA

Abraham Lincoln's Intellectual Development: 1809-1837
by Vito N. Silvestri, Ph.D. and Alfred P. Lairo

First Printing – November 2013
ISBN: 978-1-60047-919-9

Cover: Sculpture of Abraham Lincoln with Book and Ax
by Avard Fairbanks, 1953
Donated by the Sons of Utah Pioneers
New Salem, Illinois

Cover Photograph by Doug Carr, New Berlin, Illinois

Printed in the U.S.A.

0   1   2   3   4   5   6   7   8

THIS BOOK IS DEDICATED TO

I dedicate this book to Marc Silvestri and to Mimi, two special blessings in my life, to my family, sisters Elizabeth and Carmela who always encouraged me, and as always, to my beloved parents Elva and Vito Antonio Silvestri.

A special note of gratitude to Fred Lairo: a great scholar-partner, editor and writer who made this a delightful project. I'm a lucky guy.

- Vito (Vic) Silvestri

I wish to dedicate my portion of this enterprise to:

My wife Karen, my three daughters, Jennifer, Deborah and Christina, my father Pietro, my mother Jenny, my brother Alexander, my sister Vivienne, and to Dr. Silvestri for allowing me the opportunity to participate in the writing of this book.

- Alfred P. Lairo

and

To the Gift of Abraham Lincoln: His contribution to the pulse, heritage and life course of America continues to be an inspiration for us all.

Lincoln studying by the fireplace

CONTENTS

ILLUSTRATIONS

Abraham Lincoln studying by the fireplace

The cabin where Lincoln was born, Kentucky

Lincoln family cabin, Pigeon Creek, Indiana

Parental Icons

Replica of flat riverboat of the Lincoln era, Lincoln's New Salem Historic Site, IL

Replica of the Berry-Lincoln Store, Lincoln's New Salem Historic Site, IL

Surveyor Sculpture of Lincoln, Lincoln's New Salem Historic Site, IL

Replica of Miller-Kelso double cabin, Lincoln's New Salem Historic Site, IL

Abraham Lincoln on the Prairie, Lincoln's New Salem Historic Site, IL

Rendering of Lincoln as a young lawyer

The cabin where Abraham Lincoln was born:
Sinking Spring Farm, Hardin County, Kentucky
February 12, 1809

PART ONE

Initiating Self-Learning During His Growing-Up Years, Kentucky and Indiana, 1809-1830

"Abe was diligent for knowledge. [He] wished to know and if pains and labor would get it he was sure to get it.... He read all the books he could lay his hands on....

Got up early and then read.... when he came across a passage that struck him he would write it down on boards if he had no paper and keep it until he did get paper."

-Sarah Bush Lincoln, Interview by William H. Herndon, *HI,* Sept.1865, pp. 1206-107.

Lincoln on his education: (About frontier life) "There was absolutely nothing to excite ambition for education. Of course when I came of age I did not know much. Still, somehow I could read, write and cipher to the rule of three.... What little advance I have upon this store of education, I have picked up from time to time under the pressure of necessity."

-Abraham Lincoln, from his autobiographical statement for the campaign of l860.

CHAPTER ONE

Frontier Life Dispositions

From his rudimentary beginnings in a log cabin on the frontier to his achievement of the Presidency, Abraham Lincoln's life embodied the true American experience of his times. Lincoln experienced all levels of society, including, as he explained it, a temporary "slave" existence. "There is a profound correspondence," wrote Arnold Gesell, "between his peculiar genius and the pioneer culture in which he grew."[1]

For twenty-eight years, Lincoln knew what it meant to eke out a living on a frontier-farm-subsistence-economy; to work on a riverboat; to become a land surveyor; to operate a post office; to serve as a Captain in the militia; to read law and work as a law clerk; to practice law in settled communities and to make the law a reality in rural and quasi-frontier areas. Eventually, he became a state legislator, a practicing lawyer, a Representative to the United States Congress, and ultimately, the President of the United States.

Lincoln achieved this with a meager education and with a strong sense of his own mind. He used his life experiences, his limited formal education amounting to no more than one year, and the tools at his disposal: his native intelligence, a disciplined and retentive mind to develop an extraordinary ability to master content by reading, writing and speaking.

These abilities became his means to gain work beyond the physical labor of the frontier. Very early in his young life, he discovered that he could nurture his abilities and see positive results as he learned to function as a speaker, a reader and a writer.

CHAPTER TWO

A Fundamental Change of Environment

Between the ages of eight and ten years, Lincoln experienced two profound changes in his life: (1) a change in his living environment, and (2) the devastating loss of his mother, Nancy Hanks Lincoln. Ultimately these events taught him that he needed to rely solely on himself. These were excruciating developments and they became overriding premises that informed other aspects of his life.

Born on February 12, 1809, Abraham Lincoln was the first son and the second child of Nancy and Thomas Lincoln. His sister Sarah was two years older. He was born into a life of subsistence farming at Nolin Creek, Hardin County, Kentucky. Two years later the family moved to Knob Creek and to better farmland. His father owned about 348 acres.[2] They lived on the fruits of their farming, hunting and other labor. They made their own clothes, furniture, shoes, and daily faced the harsh tasks of survival as they settled onto their land and into their lives. They bartered with their neighbors and traded with merchants for whatever else they needed. All members of the family engaged in subsistence activities to maintain themselves and to prepare for the coming winters and springs.[3]

A Change in his Environment

After seven years of a relatively stable and safe environment in the frontier settlement of Knob Creek, Kentucky, the Lincoln family moved to the frontier wilderness of southern Indiana. Kentucky's lax regulations on property ownership caused a number of settlers, including Tom Lincoln, to lose their land and the homes that they had claimed, paid for and settled. Tom Lincoln lost his claims to three farms in Hardin County, Kentucky. Unable to afford an extended legal battle, Tom moved his family to southern Indiana and that met two legal criteria: (1) the land was surveyed by the US government, and (2) slavery was excluded because it was part of the Northwest Ordinance area.[4]

Abe Lincoln remembered the move to the wilderness of Indiana as one in which they had to cut their way through three miles of thickly-entangled woods to get to their site.[5] At first they lived in a three-sided cabin, or "camp," consisting of poles, brush and tree branches. The fourth side of the camp was a roaring fire. They listened to the cries of the wolves, panthers and bears at night until they could erect a log cabin.[6]

In 1816, the unsettled land was rampant with wild animals and in this part of southern Indiana; there were no settlements within a three-mile radius of their home. The Lincolns arrived on the day Indiana gained statehood, December 7, 1816, and began a fierce struggle to survive the winter. Although a log cabin was built within a few weeks, they were unable to mortar the spaces between the logs because the ground was frozen. A compound of clay and grass could not be made until early spring. The cabin was drafty and dark; they walked on a dirt floor; there were no windows and a temporary door served as an entrance.[7]

Starting over again, Thomas Lincoln and his family survived by subsisting on hunting wild animals and game. Slowly, as the weather permitted, they began to clear enough land to plant crops in the spring. Clearing the land became a continual effort for the next fourteen years. They had moved to the most chaotic, wildest and dangerous environment they had ever known. Within a few years this area became known as the Pigeon Creek Settlement of Perry County (later Spenser County). Lincoln remembered his fears in this rhyme (c.1846):

When first my father settled here,
'Twas then the frontier line:
The panther's scream, filled the night with fear
And bears preyed on the swine.[8]

Clearly the Lincolns had begun a life more impoverished than any they had experienced as a family in Kentucky.

CHAPTER THREE

The Death of Nancy Hanks Lincoln

Within two years, the frontier environment led to the death of his mother. When Tom Lincoln moved his family to southern Indiana, he did not know, nor could he know, that malaria was endemic to this area and that it also fostered the growth of poisonous plants like snakeroot. Almost every year, people in this region suffered from a mysterious and fatal illness called "the milksick." When the weather was devoid of rain, the cows ate snakeroot, a plant which stored moisture but contained a deadly poison, tremotol. This was transmitted in their milk, and it manifested itself in a trembling behavior in the cows. Adults who drank the milk from an affected cow usually died within one week.[9] No one who settled on the frontier had any knowledge of tremotol.

Death and Its Influence on Young Abe Lincoln

During the first nine years of his life, Abe experienced the death of four family members. When he was three years old, his brother Thomas died three days after his birth. When he was nine years old his mother's aunt and uncle, Elizabeth (Betsy) and Thomas Sparrow, died. They had lived near the Lincolns in Kentucky, with their nephew Dennis Hanks. Nine months later, the Sparrows lost their property, and moved, with Dennis, to the Indiana frontier next to the Lincolns. Hanks, at nineteen, was ten years older than Abe. They lived in the Lincoln's half-faced cabin until their own home could be built. Ten months later, Elizabeth and Thomas Sparrow died of the "milksick" illness. Nancy Lincoln helped to care for her Aunt and

Uncle and after they died, she helped her neighbor, Nancy Brooner (Mrs. Peter Brooner). Within a week after Mrs. Brooner died of the "milksick," Nancy was stricken with the fatal illness. At Nancy's burial Peter Brooner told Tom Lincoln, "Now, we are brothers," meaning "in the same kind of sorrow." [10]

There is no information about how the three-year-old Abe Lincoln reacted to the death of his baby brother Thomas. But the death of his mother, shortly after the deaths of his great Uncle and Aunt, had to be a profound loss. The children watched their mother nurse her relatives and then help Mrs. Brooner until their deaths. One week after they died, Nancy Lincoln became ill, and Abe and Sarah became helpless eyewitnesses who watched their mother become so weak that she could only lie on her back. Breathing shallowly and suffering an irregular pulse, she slipped into a coma and died. On her deathbed, Nancy Lincoln told young Sarah and Abe to "be good and kind to their father, to one another and to the world" and expressed the hope that they might live their lives as she had taught them to live.[11] Abe and Sarah watched their father make coffins to bury their relatives, their neighbor, and then their mother. Thomas Lincoln and Dennis Hanks sawed tree trunks into planks for coffins. Abe whittled wooden pegs for his mother's coffin.[12]

Doris Kearns Goodwin wrote that so great a loss was a transforming act for Lincoln and his sister.[13] It separated them from all they had previously known of life. Dr. Bernard Brommel, a family therapist, noted that the profundity of the loss of a parent at an early age raises key issues in children's lives: inevitably there is the fear of abandonment; the worry that they may be next to die; and the generally enveloping insecurity of their daily lives that they would have to endure in a world less certain.[14]

Thus, Nancy Hanks Lincoln's death created immediate concerns and remained as a frame of reference that changed their lives, that altered how they thought about themselves, and that influenced their relationships with others and with their own view of the world.

After the death of his Aunt and Uncle, cousin Dennis Hanks moved in with the Lincolns. Sarah Lincoln, twelve-years-old and grieving, tried to do the household chores and the cooking, and despaired that she could not measure up to her mother.[15] At age nine, Abe's duties were outside the home, in the fields, chopping trees with his ax, clearing the land, learning to make split-rail fences, helping to plant crops, and maintaining the livestock.

Fourteen months later, Sarah and Abe reached the nadir of their despair when their father left them to find a wife and stepmother. He left them in the cabin with their older cousin, nineteen-year-old Dennis Hanks. He returned to Knob Creek, Kentucky, a trip of one hundred miles that normally took five days. Accounts of this period vary but indicate that he was gone from his children from two to three months; although Burlingame estimated that it was nearly a six-month period. [16]

Abe remembered this period as the loneliest time of his life. He confided to a friend that he found solace by recalling the Bible stories his mother told him because he wanted to hear her voice in his mind, seemingly as a way to keep himself stable.[17] Impoverished by the loss of their mother and the lengthy absence of their father, living in an isolated clearing amidst dense forestation, and receiving no information about their father, Sarah and Abe eventually began to believe that a wild animal must have been killed him. [18]

Lincoln family cabin, Pigeon Creek, Indiana, 1869.
Thomas Lincoln built this house in 1817. It was without windows,
wooden floor, and a door until Sarah Bush Lincoln insisted on these
changes for their blended family.

CHAPTER FOUR

The Stabilizing Influence of Sarah Bush Lincoln

On December 2, 1819, in Elizabethtown, Kentucky, Thomas Lincoln, at the age forty-one, married Sarah Bush Johnston, at the age thirty-one. Sarah Bush Lincoln was born, married, and bore three children in Elizabethtown. Her husband Daniel Johnston died in 1816. Tom and Nancy Lincoln knew the Johnstons in the early years of their marriage in Kentucky.

When Tom, and his new wife Sarah Bush Johnston Lincoln, arrived at the Pigeon Creek homestead with her three children and two wagons-loads of household goods, they found Sarah and Abe, "ragged," dirty, wearing torn clothes, and hungry. Sarah immediately embraced them as her own children and washed and dressed them in clean clothes that she had brought with her. She wanted to make them "look more human."[19]

Sarah Bush Lincoln was "astonished" not only at the state of the children but at the primitive living conditions of her new home. She had "lived in a settled community all her life." [20] She described Indiana as "wild and desolate." [21] What she saw before her was an isolated log cabin home minimally finished and neglected, surrounded by a very dense forest, a metaphor for the state of the Lincoln family and its disintegration since the death of Nancy Lincoln.

Sarah insisted that a real door and windows be made for the cabin. She also had beds constructed for the children, one for Abe, her son John as well as for Dennis who would sleep in the loft, and another downstairs for the three girls, Sarah, Elizabeth and Matilda. The roof needed to be repaired to keep the snow from drifting into the loft. There were drafts between the logs that needed to be "chinked," closed with a grass and mud mortar. She also had the dirt floor replaced with a wooden one. And, she established special places where the children and adults could clean themselves, inside and outside the house. Within three to four weeks living conditions had improved dramatically for the Lincoln family, with their new lives under the capable guidance of Sarah Bush Lincoln.

Sarah brought bedding, mattresses, a table and chairs, household goods, cookware, dishware and eating utensils. The Lincolns had a pewter dish and some tin bowls and a few eating implements. They lived minimally because they sold most of their household furnishings before leaving Kentucky. She replaced the crude sleeping pallets made of leaves and corn shuck stuffing covered by cloth and animal skins that served as beds with warm, comfortable feathered mattresses. She owned a finely made bureau, and brought that along with a clothes chest, a spinning wheel, and extra clothes for the children. Tom Lincoln had wanted her to sell much of her furniture and household goods, but she refused. Sarah and Abe had seen few items like these in their home.[22] In effect, Sarah Bush Lincoln brought the trappings of civilization to the dense wilderness of this rough home of Tom Lincoln.

She also brought order and structure to the newly blended family. A handsome, tall woman, she became the central figure of the family, and began to establish norms to create order and cleanliness in a log cabin where eight people lived. She also nurtured relationships. She was affectionate with each child. She let Sarah and Abe know that they were her children as much as her own. Her fair-mindedness in handling all the children provided a positive climate in which they could flourish. Young Sarah Lincoln no longer had to be responsible for the entire household; she was free for tasks and responsibilities commensurate to her age and development. Her stepsisters were

Elizabeth Johnston also age twelve and Matilda Johnston age eight. Abe was ten and his stepbrother, John Johnston, was nine.

The new family of Tom Lincoln included three adults and five children. It was a family based on an underlying structure of parental loss. Thomas Lincoln was orphaned at age seven; Dennis Hanks was orphaned at age nineteen. Sarah and Abe Lincoln lost their mother at ages eleven and nine; Elizabeth, John and Matilda Johnston lost their father at ages nine, seven and five respectively.

By contrast, Sarah Bush Lincoln, the central figure of this blended family, grew up in a united family of six brothers and two sisters, and two parents who lived to see most of their children entering adulthood. As one of eight children, she came from a stable family experience that taught her the give-and-take of living with several siblings. Additionally, her three years as a single parent of her three children certainly would have sharpened her awareness of family cohesiveness, of the need to share affection and attention fairly on each child, as well as the need to recognize the individual traits which distinguished each child.

Most importantly, however, for Sarah and Abe Lincoln, their new, blended family meant that they were no longer isolated and alone. Their stepsisters and stepbrother became companions, albeit, ones who had lived a very different life in Elizabethtown. Their home was a few blocks from the courthouse of Hardin County, Kentucky. County seats were the hub of civilization in rural and frontier areas. Elizabeth, John and Matilda had different stories to tell Abe and Sarah. Abe and Sarah had country and frontier stories to tell them. In all, there was new life, a healthier animus that began to characterize the re-shaped Lincoln family in 1819.[23]

Tom and Sarah shared several areas of common ground. They had lived in the same area, and knew each other in earlier years; moreover, they both endured the death of a spouse and understood a life of poverty. Sarah lived as a single mother with three children for three years in Elizabethtown and was trying to pay her deceased husband's debts when Tom Lincoln asked her to marry him. He paid her debts before he married her.[24] She had no money at that time to send her children to school. One advantage for Sarah was that her children had more security. They also ate better food in their new frontier life with the abundance of wild game and fruit in the area. They could also attend the subscription school with Abe and Sarah. Significantly, the impact of the loss of a parent was a common denominator among the children.

So the new Mrs. Lincoln established order, cooked indoors and outdoors, cleaned, and sewed, made and washed clothes, made candles, bartered with tradesmen and other families as the area became more settled, and encouraged her children to grow and flourish.

Within a short time Sarah recognized that Abe was a uniquely bright child and loved books and learning.[25] Although she had little education herself, she had brought four books with her from Kentucky: her family Bible, Noah Webster's *The American Spelling Book*, John Bunyan's *Pilgrims' Progress* and Scott's *Lessons in Elocution*.[26] Abe read and reread these books and memorized passages and stories from them. Many years later, when Abe reflected on his growing–up years with his stepmother, he cited Sarah Bush Lincoln as one who had become "his best friend in the world...no son could love a mother more than he loved her." [27] Of his own mother, whom he referred to as his "angel mother," he told his friend Herndon that "all I am I owe to her." [28] This statement seems to be taken in the context that he inherited his intelligence, intellectual curiosity and moral teachings from Nancy Hanks Lincoln. But Lincoln also referred to his stepmother as his "sainted mother," because of the affection and encouragement she gave to him, and the stability she established for his life for eleven years in Indiana.

CHAPTER FIVE

Verbalness and the Lincoln Family: Lincoln Gains Oral and Written Literacy

The Lincoln family from its beginnings was a verbal one. Tom Lincoln, Abe's father, enjoyed a reputation as an engaging storyteller at home and at social gatherings.[29] Nancy Hanks Lincoln, Abe's birthmother, consistently described as intellectual, humorous and affectionate, enjoyed discourse with others. John Hanks, her cousin, described her as a "tall slender woman...beyond all doubts an intellectual woman, rather extraordinary if anything. Her nature was kindness, mildness, tenderness and obedience to her husband. Abraham was like his mother very much."[30]

Tom Lincoln was an athletic, robust and humorous man with an easy disposition. He was a muscular man of great endurance, five feet, ten inches, weighing 196 pounds. A farmer and a carpenter, Tom Lincoln was known as "a man who took the world easy."[31] He had almost no education but was able to read a little and to write his name. His storytelling reputation grew during his years in Indiana. William Greene, a friend of Abe Lincoln, stated that Tom Lincoln "had no superior in story telling...especially when we take into account that he was destitute of an education."[32]

Nancy Lincoln was taught to read but not to write. This was typical of the education of women at that time. She wrote an "X" for her name on legal documents.[33] Regardless, she was a seminal influence on Abe and Sarah's literacy development as well as on their moral upbringing. She read the Bible daily to her children and told biblical stories to them as she did her chores. On the frontier The Bible served as the major source of morality, and the standard for language and literature. Essentially, it played a unifying role for people to establish little civilizations on the frontier.

Dennis Hanks described the orality of their frontier culture when William Herndon asked him how Lincoln was able to learn so much in Indiana "under such disadvantages." Hanks replied, "We learned by sight and sense and hearing. We heard all that was said and talked over and over the question heard...went to political and other speeches.... We would hear all sides and opinions...discuss them, agreeing or disagreeing."[34]

Nat Grigsby, who grew up with Lincoln, said they attended political discussions: "From 1825 to 1830, the year Lincoln left for Illinois...we heard questions discussed–talked everything over and over and in fact wore it out. We learned much this way."[35]

During his early years until age seven, Lincoln was assigned chores inside and outside of the home. Frontier life developed normative patterns for children. The girls learned to do the indoor tasks of cooking, washing, sewing, cleaning, weaving, making clothing, and the outside tasks in the garden and orchard; usually the boys until the age of seven performed tasks for their mother and father in and around the house. Abe would help plant seeds from about age five for his father. Since he was taller and seemed stronger than other boys his age, his father taught him how to use an axe at the age of seven.[36] He also taught him basic carpentering skills and how to farm and attend to livestock. Typically, frontier children attended school in the winter after the harvesting ended and before the planting season began. If there were someone in the area who had a little more education than most, that person would offer a subscription school.

Nancy Lincoln prepared her children for literacy. Abe and Sarah, at their mother's encouragement, learned their ABC's when they were five years old.[37] Lincoln practiced his ABC's with a piece of charcoal on a wooden board. Reading and writing were highly prized skills in frontier life. When they could read words, she encouraged them to take turns reading a sentence or two from a biblical passage.[38] She read the Bible every day to them. On Sundays, without a church nearby, she held forth by reading aloud from the Bible and leading a related discussion.

Sarah Bush Lincoln enjoyed conversation and loved to laugh at funny stories and jokes. She also grew up in a home where politics were often discussed. She encouraged her children to attend school when they moved to Indiana. She recognized how important reading was for Abe and advocated to Tom that Abe should be allowed the time and opportunity to follow his literary inclinations. Tom wanted his children to be functional in reading and writing, but he did not always understand Abe's love of reading when there were farm chores that needed to be done. [39]

But consistently in the Lincoln home in Kentucky and their fourteen years in Indiana, discourse and formal and informal public address were the major instruments for learning, informing, adopting positions, and for changing viewpoints. Fluency in speaking was perceived as something to be admired and a way to distinguish oneself; literacy in reading and writing were advantages that could lead to better or newer life pathways.

Lincoln's Early Awakening to Verbal Behavior

From Lincoln's early formative years to his final years of life, he was enamored with words and became an astute user of the American language. He manifested this in his speaking, writing and reading. He read so thoroughly that one could trace key works he read to the kind of language or style he used in writing. Clearly, Abe Lincoln was stimulated by the orality in the Lincoln household and the practice of it at events and in churches on the frontier. He heard special accounts of his father and mother's families, especially about the Indians and the killing of Tom Lincoln's father when he was six years old, and about the kidnapping of Nancy's cousin and the family's recovery of her. These narratives along with the daily biblical stories had to encourage an early interest in speaking and in oral language.

The process of acquiring speech and language is one of imitation, encouragement from others in a child's environment, and the recognition of the necessity of language to give order to one's world. From infancy to early childhood, a child learns to assign meaning to his or her world through sensory information. In the womb, touch is a basic all-encompassing sense and an initial way of understanding for the child. Nine months of its life in the mother's womb was spent in a warm, moist and completely tactile environment, with some sound entering the womb from outside the body. At birth other senses become prominent, sight, sound, smell and taste. These senses, along with touch, become the means by which a child understands its world.

Meaningfulness for a child begins in the womb. For the newborn, the mother's touch and her body are familiar and may communicate security, since this was its primary sensory experience. The sound of the father's voice, though muffled as sound in the womb but probably heard daily after the first trimester, also becomes a source of cognition. These experiences take on major significance to the newborn. Interestingly, the pioneers in the Knob Creek region would come to see the newborn and touch the baby as a way of greeting it. Cousin Dennis Hanks, at ten years old, was the second male to touch baby Abraham. [40]

Thus, what occurs in infancy is the beginning of a lifelong process of assigning meaning to sensory data. As the brain develops the lifelong process of abstracting meaning from people, events, and the environment occurs. Through awareness, imitation, repetition, and reinforcement by significant people in the child's environment, the child gradually learns to turn random sounds into meaningful ones like "Ma-Ma" and "Da-Da". The child begins to combine sounds into words and progressively, along with its physical and neurological development, a child reaches a level of learning whereby those words become meaningfully combined as sentences, i.e., "baby eat," "dog barks." Much later, usually five to seven years, the child begins learning to transfer this oral language, speech, into written letters, words, sentences and concepts. All of this verbal behavior is a process of symbolic interaction with environment and people.

Words came to be very important in Abraham's life, certainly in his relationships with other people, in his formal education, in his legislative and law careers, and significantly in his Presidency. In his early childhood, his speaking ability, i.e., learning to say words evidently developed earlier than other children his age. His oral and aural environment must have been strongly stimulated daily by his mother and by his sister Sarah, two years older, and consequently more advanced in speech than her brother. Additionally, his father, when he returned from his labors, was in the habit of telling stories after dinner, and at special events, perhaps not daily, but it was still a significant oral activity for the child to observe and to learn. It seems clear that the Lincoln family created an environment in early childhood conducive to encouraging and accelerating Abe's learning of speech and language acquisition.

Nancy Lincoln told two-year old Sarah words and stories from the Bible and Lincoln would have become aware of this behavior as he and Sarah grew and advanced in their early formative years. The mother and sister's verbalness would act as stimuli for him to imitate. Dennis Hanks said she "repeated" the stories "to Abe and his sister when very young... Lincoln was often very much moved by the stories." [41] His mother and father talking to each other and conversing with visiting neighbors and other adults provided examples of verbal behavior to emulate. Gradually Abe learned, like every child that speaking and listening and performing these behaviors elicited rewards, met his needs, validated him and reinforced his verbal messages.

Visually, he learned that verbal behavior could also occur as a result of a book, in this case, the Bible that his mother read aloud daily to them. Later, during his fifth year, his mother added the making of letters, an activity of refined hand-eye coordination to her teaching. Dennis Hanks noted that she encouraged her children to practice the making of the alphabet again and again. This was a quiet activity, one that Abe engaged in diligently. He often made his letters with a piece of charcoal on a clean piece of board. Dennis Hanks claimed to have taught Abe how to use a quill pen he made from a buzzard's feather by placing his hand over the child's and guiding it to form written letters. [42]

Nancy Lincoln's early intellectual nourishment by her skill instruction, her stories and the lessons from their Bible established a dimension of learning beyond the pressing physical necessities of daily work to survive in the wilderness of southern Indiana. Moreover, a continual growth pattern of verbal behavior is universal to any newborn child. Gesell noted this verbalness helped Lincoln to "come by his mind as he came by his body through deep-seated mechanisms of growth." [43]

CHAPTER SIX

Reading, Writing and Ciphering in Kentucky

Lincoln remembered his early schooling in Kentucky: "My sister and I were sent for short periods, to ABC school, the first kept by Zachariah Riney, and the second by Caleb Hazel." [44] Anyone who could read and write and "cipher" to the "rule of three" could establish a subscription school. The rule of three was a means of determining the fourth term in a proposition when three terms were given. Samuel Haycraft, a citizen of the Knob Creek area, knew Hazel and said that besides Hazel's physical size which would intimidate students and maintain order, he could not go beyond teaching the basics.[45]

The backbone of the elementary curriculum was centered on Dilworth's *Speller,* also known as *A New Guide to the English Tongue: In Five Parts* (1747). Students learned to speak, read and write words, phrases and sentences. Grammar sections and literary excerpts from the Psalms and the Bible were also part of this textbook.[46] Twelve pages of this textbook were devoted to "A Moral Catechism," a section written as a dialectic on great virtues and poor motives, i.e. reverence, humility, generosity, avarice, etc. A question was asked and an answer was provided: "Is justice easy to know?" and the reply provided is "Where there is any difficulty in determining, consult the golden rule." [47]

Lincoln often referred to his formal education as "blab schools" because they were strongly grounded in oral communication. Every morning students individually recited their homework before the instructor. The teaching method of "blab" schools was to keep the children engaged. Quietness in the classroom signified slackness. Students also read aloud daily, learned to pronounce new words, to speak, print and write the alphabet and to copy phrases and sentences from the book. Once or twice a week there was a spelling bee. The learning of words advanced from monosyllabic to more complex syllabic combinations with sample readings corresponding to the level of learning to be gained: for example, these monosyllabic statements: "No man may put off the law of God," and "Now I lay me down to sleep." [48]

Frontier subscription schools often lasted from a few weeks to three months, and parents paid a fee from $1.50 to $2.00 per child.[49] Dennis Hanks stated that Abe and Sarah attended school about three months at the most in Kentucky before they moved to Indiana.[50] After Lincoln attended the formal school, there is some indication that Abe may have received tutorial help from his second teacher, Caleb Hazel. Hazel lived near the Lincoln home and his second wife was related to Nancy Lincoln. Hazel also was strong on teaching students clear penmanship and it is believed that Abe learned this from Hazel not only in formal sessions but also in tutorials afterward.[51]

Abe's brief formal school in Kentucky had certainly helped him to refine his mastery of basic reading and writing that Nancy Lincoln had begun. He often practiced writing words and sentences, scrawling words with charcoal on any material around, boards, sand, and writing in snow, all of which helped him to improve his ability to write. Described as a "tall spindle of a boy" at the age of seven, he did well in school and developed a reputation for solitude during playtime periods in the school day, a pattern that became more pronounced as he matured.[52] Several of the Lincolns' illiterate neighbors were impressed with Lincoln's literacy at this age.[53]

CHAPTER SEVEN

Reading and Studying: Maintaining the Process of Self-Learning

"He (Abe) had a great memory and for hours he would tell me what he had read"

-Henry Brooner, boyhood friend of Abe Lincoln [54]

At the age of seven, when the Lincolns came to the wilderness frontier of Indiana, Abe brought a basic ability to read and write to the frontier life. After learning basic reading skills, Abe began his unquenchable life-long pursuit of reading to learn. Nearly four years would go by before Abe and Sarah would attend formal schooling again.

Self-learning evolved, especially on long winter days when his chores were completed. The Bible was a constant source of reading for them. It was also a nurturing resource for right conduct and explanations about the world. The Bible served as an active element in their lives, with daily readings, and more importantly, with the added material in the Lincoln family Bible. In addition to the traditional text, their edition also included "arguments prefixed to the different books and moral and theological observations." [55] These were topics for family discussions especially on Sunday when Nancy Lincoln devoted part of the day for Bible reading, study and discussion, in the absence of a church in the Little Pigeon Creek area. Thomas Lincoln, often described as an honest and moral man, would have encouraged such a practice. A few years later, as the region began to settle, he had the chief responsibility of supervising the building of a Baptist church. Abe assisted him on this.[56]

For Abe and Sarah, the Bible was their best example of the English language. Its measured sentence structure was clear, word choice relatively simple, and stylistically, the parallel structure of its statements and the abundance of narratives to teach a moral provided their most consistent exposure to a higher level of English.

Sarah and Abe also continued to study Dilworth's *Spelling Book,* which gave them the opportunity to improve their language skills and to advance to higher levels of reading. Moreover, the Bible was a book that required re-reading as it was a service book for religious teachings. This may have been the impetus for Abe to re-read books for greater meaning and understanding. From his reading, Abe developed the practice of writing words, sentences and statements he wanted to remember in a copybook. If he didn't have paper, he would write it on clean pieces of board and recopy his work onto paper later.

Evidently Abe had practiced his handwriting sufficiently so that his penmanship was clear and readable. After the family moved to Indiana, he became the family's correspondent. Within two years, as more Kentuckians from the Knob Creek area moved into Pigeon Creek, many of them asked Abe to write letters for them to send to their relatives.[57] He engaged in this practice as a scribe for his neighbors for eleven years. Reflecting on his letter-writing activities in Indiana, Abe told Mentor Graham, a friend and tutor to him during his New Salem years, that he came to understand other people's thoughts and feelings by learning to put their sentiments into written language. [58]

Between the ages of eleven and fifteen Abe's reading included the following, in this progression: *Arabian Nights, Aesop's Fables,* Daniel *Depoe's The Life and Adventures of Robinson Crusoe,* Paul Bunyan's *A Pilgrim's Progress,* William Scott's *Lessons in Elocution,* Weems' *Life of Washington,* and *The Autobiography of Benjamin Franklin. Arabian Nights, Aesop's Fables and Robinson Crusoe* were books which would appeal to Lincoln as a young adolescent because of their worlds of fantasy and adventure. It also brought into his life an imaginary world exotically different from the harshness of frontier life.

Aesop's Fables and *Pilgrim's Progress* were anchored strongly in moral lessons. *Aesop's Fables* often had lessons very similar to the *Bible,* with the most notable narrative ending with the precept that "A house divided against itself cannot stand."

Weems' biography of George Washington was a romantic and idealistic presentation. This had the appeal of meeting a young person's need for heroes who seemed larger than ordinary life.

The more realistic *Autobiography of Benjamin Franklin* might have had importance for Lincoln as a significant statement of a life in Colonial America about someone who was without advantages like himself, but was a person who could build a prosperous life that also led to serving the nation.

A few years later, Abe read David Ramsey's *Life of George Washington,* which provided a fuller account of Washington's life and the Revolutionary War. He had borrowed this book from Josiah Crawford and it had become damaged by rain while in his possession. Abe had no money to pay Crawford, but offered to work for him for the full value of the book. Crawford needed to have the tops of his corn stalks cut as it provided winter fodder for his cattle. Lincoln recalled this incident when he was an eighteen year old: "You see," he said, "I am tall and long-armed, and I went to work in earnest. At the end of two days there was not a corn-blade left on a stalk in the field. I wanted to pay full damage for all the wetting the book got, and I made a clean sweep." [59] When he finished making restitution, Crawford told him to keep the book. As with every book Lincoln read and owned, "he read, re-read and studied it thoroughly." [60]

Along with Weems' *George Washington,* William Scott's *Lessons in Elocution* may have been among the most important books Lincoln read and studied in his early teen years. It seems that *Lessons in Elocution* gave him his first introduction to the plays of Shakespeare. Thereafter, Lincoln maintained a life-long interest in Shakespeare's works. Moreover, he began to study public speaking through this book as well as to study it from the preachers he heard. Essentially, *Lessons on Elocution* was a book on how to speak and perform in public. It included instructions on how to use and develop one's speaking voice, how to gesture, prescriptive ways to present eighty-one emotional states to an audience, as well as literary excerpts for practice, memorization and declamation.

Eleven soliloquies were included from Shakespeare's plays: three from *Hamlet,* including his advice to the players and his soliloquy on death; three from *Julius Caesar,* including Antony's oration over Caesar's body; five from *Henry IV;* one from *Richard III;* and one from *As You Like It,* i.e., *"All the world's a stage...";* Cato's speech on Immortality from Joseph Addison's *Tragedy of Cato* also was included.

Several quotations were also part of the excerpted material, most notably the following that pertained to Lincoln's development and life:

> "... there is nothing truly valuable which can be purchased without pains and labor: *Tattler;*

> "You must love learning if you would possess it," Knox;

> "Whatever you pursue, be emulous to excel," Blair.[61]

These three quotations are synchronous with Sarah Bush Lincoln's observation about him. Abe, she said, "could easily learn and long remember, and when he did learn anything he learned it well and thoroughly." [62]

At the age of fifteen, his final period of formal schooling, Lincoln's teacher was Azel Dorsey, the most educated teacher he had to this time. The Lincolns knew the Dorsey family in Kentucky. Azel Dorsey served as Commissioner of Revenue Tax for Hardin County. He moved to Indiana between 1813 and 1816 and served as election clerk in Warrick County, Indiana, Treasurer of Spenser County in Rockport, and his house served as headquarters for county officers. Later he served as county coroner. Dorsey taught in the Little Pigeon Creek area at the school erected by the settlers. [63]

Dorsey is reported to have said to Chauncey Hobart that Lincoln was "one of the noblest boys I ever knew, and . . . certain to become noted if he lives." [64] Dorsey evidently taught Lincoln arithmetic during this period. Lincoln had come to school with an old textbook, Pike's *Arithmetic*, and Dorsey taught at least to the "rule of three." According to Abe, Tom Lincoln thought that a mastery of "'ciperin clean through the 'rithmetic" was the highest education his son could attain.[65] Lincoln studied from this book and continued working on math problems long after his schooling ended. Warren, who reviewed Lincoln's copybook containing his math problems and who had inspected Pike'*s Arithmetic,* believed that Lincoln gained a strong foundation in mathematics.

Two years later, in 1826 at the age of seventeen when he no longer attended school, Lincoln was working on advanced problems beyond the rule of three. Isaac N. Arnold, a lawyer friend and early biographer of Lincoln, owned a few pages of Lincoln's copybook that had his computation of discount and interest exercises. First, he wrote the definition of discounting, then he cited the rules for its computation, and finally he developed proofs and examples. He followed the same problem solving procedures for computing interest.[66]

When Abe's schooling ended he had met the standards of a "common-school" education within the laws of Indiana. Essentially, this was at least "one year's schooling in the English language" according to Indiana law. [67]

No known picture exists of Nancy Hanks Lincoln

Nancy Hanks Lincoln	Thomas Lincoln*	Sarah Bush Lincoln**
1784 – 1818	1778 – 1851	1788 – 1869

PARENTAL ICONS

Nancy Hanks Lincoln, Thomas Lincoln and **Sarah Bush Lincoln** set Abe on a course towards independence, intellectual development and *well-grounded ethical perspectives.*

Nancy Hanks Lincoln, Abe's birth mother, was known for her intellectual curiosity and this translated to her children's early development with her daily recitations of biblical stories, her daily oral readings of the Bible, and her encouragement of literacy. Moreover for moral and economic reasons, she and Tom Lincoln were of one mind in their opposition to slavery.

Thomas Lincoln, not able to read very much, acknowledged the need for education, encouraged Abe to study mathematics, sent him and his daughter Sarah first in Kentucky and later his three step-children to subscription school in Indiana. Moreover, his ability to speak well and tell stories, and his example as an upright citizen who earned the respect of his neighbors served as an *instructive example* for Abraham.

Sarah Bush Lincoln was impressed with Abe's intellect and sensed that be would be walking a different life journey. She encouraged and often became an advocate for Abe to be allowed to read and study. She remained a staunch advocate and affectionate friend to him, and he knew he could rely on her support. In effect she *validated him* by giving him permission to study, read and follow his interests

By example, all three parents demonstrated to a young Lincoln, that by daily hard work, often against harsh conditions, by not giving up when beaten down, and by investing in himself toward future gratification, a person could yield results and help to sustain one's life and ambitions. Perhaps, even more important, all three parents subscribed to the teachings of the Bible and the idea of government by the people.

So, Abraham Lincoln, straight from the frontier, with book and axe, along with a deep understanding of biblical and other moral teachings, stepped boldly into public life, "with malice towards none" to fulfill his destiny.

* - Photographer *I* document courtesy of the Abraham Lincoln Library and Museum of Lincoln Memorial University, Harrogate, Tennessee.

** - From the Lincoln Financial Foundation Collection, courtesy of The Indiana State Museum and Allen County Public Library.

CHAPTER EIGHT

Becoming a Self-Learner and Becoming a Hired Hand

Lincoln continued to maintain his strong interest in reading. His post-school reading included two additional books on elocution, A.T. Lowe's *The Columbian Class Book* and *The Kentucky Preceptor,* a new edition of Caleb Bingham's *The American Preceptor.* He also studied dictionaries, notably Nathan Bailey's *A Universal Etymological English Dictionary.* This dictionary provided the origin and history of words. Bailey's *Dictionary* was also available to him in the Lincoln home.[68]

The most unusual book he studied, when he was twenty years old, was *The Revised Laws of Indiana [1824]... to which are prefixed the Declaration of Independence, the Constitution of The United States, and the Constitution of the State of Indiana.* David Turnham, his friend and neighbor, lent him this book and noted that Lincoln spent hours and hours studying it.[69] It was his first reading of the *Constitution.* He may have read *The Declaration of Independence* earlier in the newspapers. Regardless these documents were certain to resonate as part of his education and as part of his adult life. Before he read the *Revised Laws* Lincoln had heard some notable lawyers plead their cases at court trials in county seats about fifteen miles from his home.[70] Court trials also served as a form of entertainment to early settlers.

Newspapers became available about 1826 in the Pigeon Creek area. Lincoln's stepmother said Abe was a "constant reader" of newspapers from 1827 to 1830.[71] He was able to read newspapers that were mailed to Gentry's store and Post Office. James Gentry established his store at the crossroads of a road from Rockport to Bloomington that intersected at right angles to a slightly older road from Evansville to Corydon about a mile and a half from the Lincoln farm. According to Warren's research, the following newspapers were available to Lincoln: Corydon *Gazette* (Corydon was the capital of Indiana at that time); Vincennes *Western Sun;* New Harmony *Gazette;* Terre Haute *Western Register;* Indianapolis *Gazette* and *Journal.*[72] Abe also read *The Telescope,* a New York paper (published during this period) that he borrowed from his neighbor, William Wood.

Becoming a Hired Hand

"My father taught me to work, but he never learned me to like it," said Abraham Lincoln. Between the ages of fifteen to twenty-one years, Abe spent his days laboring in the fields and being hired out to neighboring farmers. Known for his strength and for his ability to work hard, he was also known as one who took breaks in order to read. When he left to work in the fields he held his ax in one hand and his book in the other. He worked frequently for the Gentry and Crawford families, and they occasionally lent him books to read. He usually earned twenty-five cents a day and that was paid to his father. By law he could not earn money for himself until he became twenty-one.[77] In retrospect, Abe observed, "I was a slave once myself."

At the age of forty-six, Tom Lincoln had become blind in one eye and could not work as hard as before. He also relied on his stepson, John, to help support the remaining family of six after Dennis Hanks married Elizabeth Johnston. Elizabeth Crawford observed that Tom Lincoln performed his carpenter work by feel as much as he did with the sight left in his one remaining eye. [78]

In his late teens, Abe had more opportunities to be away from the Lincoln farm, not only because of his hired jobs, but also, because of the existence of Gentry's store. He would spend time talking with people, and occasionally spend early evenings there. It became a gathering place for the settlers in the Pigeon Creek area, and Lincoln established himself as an entertaining storyteller and conversationalist, much like his father.[79]

He discovered work opportunities on the Ohio River as a ferryman taking people across the Anderson River, a tributary before the larger Ohio River. He did this for a season for James Taylor who operated a packinghouse and a ferry. Abe worked odd jobs for Taylor, operated the ferry for passengers, lived with the Taylors and helped them in their home and in the fields.[80]

From eleven to nineteen, Lincoln enjoyed a normal boyhood on the frontier. He was known not only for his mental acuity, his voracious reading, his ability to explain complex ideas clearly, and his storytelling, but also, he was known for his physical prowess. Always taller than his peers and strengthened by heavy daily work with an ax or farm labor, he developed a reputation as an accomplished wrestler and fighter. If necessary, Abe used his long arms and legs to strategically pinion his opponent. He often excelled at contests in lifting heavy objects. At fifteen he was six feet in height; at nineteen he had achieved his full height, six feet and four inches. He was also considered awkward, gawky, and different because of his skinny appearance. Adolescent girls giggled about his appearance and paid attention to other boys.[81]

Two Major Events at Nineteen: Death of Sarah Lincoln Grigsby and a Trip to New Orleans

The Death of Sarah Lincoln Grigsby

At nineteen, two events occurred that could be considered markers in Abe's young life. His sister Sarah died in childbirth during her second year of marriage to Aaron Grigsby. It was a blow that devastated Lincoln. He had lost his only blood sibling and the closest person he knew in his growing up years. In many ways she was his anchor during his adolescent years. Prone to melancholy nearly all his life, Lincoln suffered as severe a depression and despondency as he had experienced with the death of his mother. Sarah's death brought on the remembered grief of the loss of his mother.[82] J.W. Lamar, who knew Lincoln at this time, said that "They were close companions, and were a great deal alike in temperament.... From then on he was alone in the world." [83]

Anger at the Grigsby family was also a part of his grief, for he blamed them for letting Sarah labor too long before a doctor could be summoned for her. She was buried with her dead child in the Little Pigeon Creek churchyard.

First Trip to New Orleans

Later that year, James Gentry asked Abe to accompany his son Allen on a flatboat trip to New Orleans. He was paid eight dollars a month. He and Allen manned a flatboat of supplies to be traded en route on the Mississippi at various plantations and then to sell everything, including the boat, in New Orleans. They were to return by steamer to Rockport, Indiana, their point of embarkation for this adventure.[84]

It was the first time Lincoln saw a city, the first time he was truly beyond the environs of the frontier life of Southern Indiana, and the first trip he made on a steamboat. As such, it served as an antidote for his grief and depression. In October 1828, he and Allen began building the flatboat. In late December, with the boat fully laden, they embarked on a 1222-mile trip from Rockport to New Orleans. Every day the two men manned the boat on its course down the Mississippi, passing miles of dense forests and stopping at known plantations to trade their corn, bacon, skins, and other farm products for cotton, tobacco and sugar.

Under Attack

After an afternoon of trading on a plantation about six miles south of Baton Rouge, they decided to anchor the flatboat. Seven Negroes, planning to kill and rob them, attacked them with clubs while they were sleeping. Allen and Abe fought them off, grabbed the clubs from some of them, threw others in the water, and then Allen shouted, "Abe, get the guns and shoot them!" With that, the Negroes ran off. There were no guns onboard, but it was a ruse that worked and the two men, wounded but alive, quickly left in the middle of the night to continue down river to New Orleans.[85] Lincoln sustained a scar on his forehead from that event. The years Lincoln had spent in improving his skills in fighting and wrestling for sport helped to save his life.

In New Orleans, once they sold their goods and their boat, the two men spent a few days sightseeing in this exotic town. New Orleans offered a variety of trading and goods, very different living conditions than Lincoln knew and a diverse language community with its different ethnic groups. Inevitably, they happened upon the slave auction. Allen Gentry recalled how angry Lincoln became when he saw this. The Negro attack they had endured had little influence on Lincoln's sense of injustice. He is reported to have sworn, "If I ever get a chance to hit this thing, I'll hit it hard." [86]

CHAPTER TEN

Facing Another Frontier

Late in the fall of 1829, a few months before his twenty-first birthday, Lincoln began preparations to leave home. A key part of his plan was to build a better home for his father and stepmother, to help them live more comfortably as they became older. He felled trees and prepared logs for a new cabin. Tom Lincoln, now fifty-one years old, helped him to erect the new cabin.[87] It became a home the Lincolns would never occupy.[88]

A few years before, John Hanks had moved to Illinois, near the village of Decatur. He wrote glowingly about the rich, fertile plains available. Dennis Hanks traveled to the area and decided to move his family to this land that was clear and "prepared for the plow." [89] Almost simultaneously while the new cabin was in construction, the Lincoln-Johnston family began making plans to leave the Pigeon Creek area. Dennis Hanks and Squire Hall, who had married Sarah and Matilda, Sarah B. Lincoln's two daughters, decided to make the move. Sarah Lincoln, who did not want to be separated from her daughters and grandchildren, convinced Tom to make the move. At this point in its development the family was less Lincoln than it was Johnston. Additionally, the milksick was especially deadly that year in the Pigeon Creek area and that was an immediate factor that contributed to the decision.[90]

Because of this development, Abe, at the age of twenty-one, remained with the family to help them to become settled on the new lands of Illinois. They embarked on March 30, 1830, with three wagons carrying thirteen family members and their goods.

John Hanks had prepared logs on land he had selected for Tom and Sarah and John Johnston, a few miles northwest of the village of Decatur. Abe, John Hanks and others erected cabins for the Lincolns and for the others. John and Abe also built a split rail fence to enclose the fifteen acres of the Lincoln homestead.[91] The Lincolns spent about a year in this area and experienced the harshest winter they had ever known. They decided to relocate. They tried two other sites before they settled near Charleston, Illinois, at Gooseneck Prarie.[92]

Abe continued to hire himself out to other farmers in the area. On one of his jobs, he split a thousand fence rails during the winter for a Major William Warnick in Macon County.[93] The following Spring, Denton Offutt, a business entrepreneur, engaged John Hanks, Abe and his step-brother, John, to build a flatboat to ship and sell goods down the Mississippi to New Orleans, embarking on this in the Spring of 1831. Once again, in New Orleans, Lincoln witnessed the slave auction. Denton Offutt, John Johnston, and Lincoln completed the trip to New Orleans. John Hanks left them in St. Louis because he was away from his family longer than he had expected.[94]

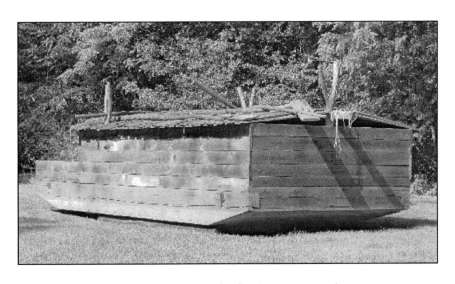

Lincoln era replica of a flat bottom riverboat
Lincoln's New Salem Historic Site, Illinois

PART TWO

Refining His Self-Learning to Establish a Career: Illinois, 1831-1837

"I have taught in my life four to six thousand pupils as schoolmaster and no one has ever surpassed him (Lincoln) in rapidity, quickly and well acquiring the rudiments and rules of English grammar. This...in the spring, summer and fall of l833."

-Mentor Graham quoted in *Mentor Graham* The Man who Taught Lincoln, K. Duncan and D.F. Nickols, (Un. of Chicago Press, 1944) pp.128-129.

Bowling Green thought Abraham Lincoln was good material and only wanted education. Bowling Green helped Lincoln during a deep depression, and mentored him on politics, the law and courtroom procedure.

-See Abner Ellis, HI, pp 173; Jason Duncan, HI, p. 540. *HI*

"Beginning as a stump orator and corner-grocery debater, he lived to take his place in the front rank of immortal orators."

-Allen Thorndike Rice, ed., *Reminisces of Abraham Lincoln* (Haskell House Publishers, 1971(originally published in 1888).

CHAPTER ELEVEN

Abe Lincoln at Twenty-One: Self-Learning and Life Experiences: Physical, Intellectual and Emotional

Abraham Lincoln lived his first twenty-one years in the expanding frontiers of Kentucky, Indiana, and Illinois. He worked in the fields and woods nearly everyday of his twenty-one years. "I was raised to farming," he said, but "my father never learned me to like it."[95]

Lincoln's Physical Development

Physically, he grew to a height of six feet, four inches, and he weighed about 175 pounds. Gangly with long arms and legs, his muscles were sinewy and strong, with unusually large hands. During his adolescent years, he became confident of his physical ability and strength. Daily hard work had strengthened him. He became an expert at wielding an ax, felling trees, chopping wood and building log cabins. "My, how he could chop," noted Hanks. "His axe would flash and bite into a sugartree or sycamore, and down it would come. If you heard him fellin' trees in a clearin,' you would say these were three men at work by the way the trees fell." [96]

He also competed in sporting contests, excelling in wrestling. "Abe was a 'rassler.... I was ten years older but I couldn't rassle him down. His legs was too long for me to throw him," said Dennis Hanks. More importantly, Abe could defend himself and saved his life when he and Allen Gentry were attacked by seven Negroes while moored on a flatboat on the way to New Orleans.

At the age of twenty-one, Abe could also perform rough carpentry, plow a field and take care of farm animals. He knew how to build a flatboat, to operate a ferry across a river, and to steer a flatboat down the Mississippi River. He could also clerk in a general store. One could say that Lincoln's physical abilities, skills and frontier life experience would be sufficient to allow him to remain as he was and settle into a productive life in a frontier town. His father, orphaned at an early age, had followed this path and was satisfied. But both father and son understood that at twenty-one, Abe had a different, but unspecified, ambition that went beyond a frontier existence.

Abe Lincoln's Mental Development: Intellect

Early in his life Abraham discovered his intellectual ability. *"I was slow to learn and slow to forget what I learned—my mind is like a piece of steel, very hard to scratch anything on it and almost impossible to after you get it there to rub it out."* [98] At some point he recognized that he needed to sharpen his intellectual skills as he became involved in the thoughts of others as well as in his own capacity to think. Throughout his developmental years he consistently sharpened his retentive skills and refined his intellectual skills of reasoning and disciplined study.

He became a self-learner. In the absence of regular formal education and because of a paucity of books, Abe learned to rely upon his own mental resources. Manual labor, plowing and harvesting fields, and all the other physical survival skills he performed daily for twenty-one years, did not have the same power for him as reading and thinking. He sought greater information and understanding, and knowledge of a wider world of possibilities that far surpassed the rudiments of frontier life. Reading, meditation, discourse with others, and self-teaching helped him to strengthen his analytical powers.

His physical gains complemented his self-confidence and his belief in his intellectual ability. It fostered an assurance about himself that he had survival skills. The challenge for Lincoln was to exercise his mind and make new intellectual discoveries by reading and studying. He not only read a book, he sought *to master it.* When he could retain its contents, speak about it to others, and write about it, then he had absorbed the wisdom of what he read and studied. Matilda Johnston Moore, Abe's youngest stepsister stated Lincoln's priorities during his growing-up years: "Abe was not energetic except in one thing: he was active and persistent in learning." [99]

Intellectually he seemed to have inherited a disposition from his mother to be curious, to ask questions, and to seek answers. Nancy Hanks Lincoln, consistently described as a woman of intellect, "known for the strength of her mind," nurtured her children to be intellectually curious. [100] As a young boy, Abe had to learn not to interrupt adult conversation with his questions. After his father punished him for interrupting, he learned to ask questions in private, when the adults had ended their conversation. He described this strong curiosity years later in an interview with Rev. John P. Gulliver:

"Among my earliest recollections...when a mere child," said Lincoln, "I used to get irritated when anybody talked to me in a way I could not understand. I don't think I ever got angry at anything else in my life. But that always disturbed my temper, and has ever since. I can remember going to my little bedroom, after hearing the neighbors talk of an evening, with my father, and spending no small part of the night walking up and down, and trying to make out what was the exact meaning of some of their, to me, dark sayings. I could not sleep...when I got on such a hunt after an idea until I had caught it; and when I thought I got it, I was not satisfied until I had repeated it over and over, until I had put it in language plain enough, as I thought, for any boy I knew to comprehend. "

To Lincoln it was a "kind of passion...that has stuck with me; for I am never easy now, when I am handling a thought, till I have bounded it north and bounded it south...east...west." [101] Lincoln's response indicated more about his mental processes than it did his education.

Gesell, in appraising Lincoln's development, emphasized the importance of his strong interest in reading and meditation. At the age of eight Abe was reading the Bible; at the age of twelve he was able to exhibit conceptual thinking from reading Weems' *Life of Washington.* In 1861, in a speech to the New Jersey Senate, Lincoln recalled that as a young boy reading the "account of the battlefields and struggles for the liberties of the country," he sensed that "there must have been something more than common that those men struggled for." [102]

Lincoln's ability to sense a larger idea from his reading experience at the age of twelve marked, for Gesell, one of the initial pieces of evidence demonstrating that he was able to understand abstract concepts at an early age. Gesell observed that Lincoln's "genius" developed through recurring periods of sheer meditation" throughout his growing-up years. [103] In his later years Lincoln taught himself advanced arithmetic and some geometry based on Euclid. The breadth of his reading began to nurture his reasoning skills that led him to read and reread the *Revised Laws of Indiana, The Constitution* and *The Bill of Rights of the United States.*

Lincoln's "passion" impelled him to think of a life beyond the frontier. The more he learned, the greater the consideration of other options for himself. Some observers and scholars state that Lincoln was ambitious. Certainly, this was an observable trait in the young Lincoln. Dennis Hanks, however, would have called it Lincoln's inheritance from his father, who had survived a harsh upbringing and was known as a man of strong will. [104] Lincoln, seemingly in jest, frequently told his peers as well as his sister that he was going to be the President of the United States. [105]

Lincoln's Emotional Development

At twenty-one, Lincoln's emotional development manifested itself in a mix of behaviors: his desire for solitude; his depressive state, often called melancholia; his joyous and funster companionship with his peers who were recipients of his humor, jokes, and storytelling; his ambivalence about himself and his relationship with women his own age during his adolescent years, as well as his ambivalence about his relationship with his father.

Lincoln evidently found comfort and stability in quiet moments each day. He awoke to read before the firelight of the kitchen hearth, and he looked forward to reading after a day of labor, before he went to sleep each night.[106] It was his time to think, to exercise his mental abilities, and to discover more ideas and gain more understanding about the nature of things. In this way, through habitual study and reflection, Lincoln created an active intellectual stability for himself.

He had no such stability emotionally

His growing–up years from nine to twenty-one seem encompassed by first the death of his mother when he was nine and the death, ten years later, of his sister Sarah when he was nineteen. He had lost the two most powerful influences on his young life, people who gave him special affection, understanding, direction and support, people who knew him from birth. The third woman in his life was his stepmother, Sarah Bush Lincoln who recognized that his journey in life would be different from the frontier options before him. She loved him, encouraged him to study, and she developed a special relationship with him that was mutually loving.

All three women in Lincoln's early years were intelligent women. Nancy Lincoln taught by precept and example. Her moral narratives from the Bible were daily teachings to her children. She taught Sarah and Abe that the Bible was the key resource in their lives for morality, for values and for making judgments. To her, the Bible was the mainstay for understanding one's position in a chaotic world.

By her daily example Nancy Lincoln also taught her children. Amidst the pressing needs to meet the immediate necessities of each day for her family, food, clothing, an ordered home, etc., governed by the need for physical labor each day to meet survival needs, Nancy Lincoln also presented a model of one who could find time in each day for Bible study and reflection. It was part of the day, and she demonstrated this example for intellectual reflection as part of one's daily life. Additionally, she taught her children that learning to read and write were key tools to developing their minds. Interestingly, Nat Grigsby said that Nancy "was superior to her husband in every way. She was a brilliant woman." [107]

Sarah Bush Lincoln recognized Abe's need for reflection and she often served as an advocate for him, interceding on his behalf to Tom Lincoln to allow Abe to read and study each day.

Moreover, both women were affectionate toward their children, building a base of love and approval. With these two role models, Nancy Lincoln in his early childhood and Sarah B. Lincoln during his adolescent and early adult years, Abe was able to flourish.

His sister, Sarah Lincoln, frequently described as similar to Abe in intellectual curiosity and humor, was also known for her warmth and outgoing cordiality to others. She and Abe shared two very significant and close bonding experiences when they were faced with the death of their mother, and the profound sense of abandonment and loneliness that they felt when their father left them in the Indiana wilderness with Dennis Hanks and went to Kentucky to re-marry.

During their adolescent years, his sister Sarah was the one person Abe could depend on. They had similar experiences. She also was hired-out for domestic work during these years. Until she married, Sarah tended to look out for Abe. They had shared the same life-journey. When she died, no one remained who had accepted and understood him all his life.

Interestingly, the numbing persistence of grief is a relevant factor for a person like Lincoln who lived close to nature throughout his first twenty-one years of life. One could argue that he witnessed life, death, and rebirth everyday he was out of the home. The omnipresent wilderness and frontier would have presented that to him. On the frontier, one could expect lives to end earlier than in more civilized places. This rationale would have offered cold comfort to Lincoln. He knew what such a powerful loss of his mother and sister meant to him. (Five years later, with the death of Ann Rutledge, Lincoln seriously considered committing suicide.[108])

Although, unproven, Lincoln may have inherited a bio-chemical disposition toward the melancholy most observers uniformly apply to descriptions of Lincoln.

Charles Strozier and Michael Burlingame suggested that Abe never sufficiently mourned the loss of his mother and that all that suppressed grief was rekindled when Sarah died.[109] Certainly Abe was closer to his mother and his sister than to anyone else in his early life. Biographer, David Donald, believed that Lincoln "unlocked an emotional barrier" when he visited the gravesites in Pigeon Creek, Indiana, on a Whig campaign trip to that region, fifteen years after he left.[110] Lincoln wrote a poem about his sadness, *My Childhood Home I See Again,* "Where things decayed, and loved ones lost, / In dreamy shadows rise." He sent it to a law friend and literary editor, Andrew Johnston, in Quincy, Illinois. Writing of his visit to this area "where my mother and sister were buried," Lincoln stated that it "aroused feelings in me which were certainly poetry" although the Pigeon Creek area was "as unimportant as any spot on earth" to be inspirational.[111] Written in four-line stanzas, Lincoln noted that he had "a deal of trouble to finish it." Johnston published the poem in the Quin*cy Whig,* May 5, 1847.

> I range the fields with pensive tread,
> And pace the hollow rooms;
> And feel (companions of the dead)
> I'm living in the tombs.

The trip awakened another trauma of his boyhood, the sudden insanity of Matthew Gentry that he had witnessed when he was fifteen. He devoted twelve stanzas to this.[112] Abe had thought of Matthew Gentry as a bright young man.[113] "How fearful are the signs displayed, / By pangs that kill the mind!" On his return to Pigeon Creek he saw Matthew Gentry again, alive and deranged, and the tragedy of his madness awakened another sorrow in him. In those stanzas, he was mourning the cruel death of reason in Matthew, and he was sorrowing about the insanity that continued to imprison his life.

Lincoln acknowledged his own roots in the stubble fields of Pigeon Creek.

> The very spot where grew the bread
> That formed my bones, I see.
> How strange, old field, on thee to tread,
> And feel I'm part of thee! [114]

Lincoln's poem while it has an authentic voice also can be read as an emotional autobiography of traumas remembered from his youth.

Abe's Ambivalence about his Father

As an example for his son, Tom Lincoln basically was a good man, known for his decency and moral conduct in the Pigeon Creek community. He was not known as an enterprising man. Essentially, he was a frontiersman. Once he established his life pattern in Pigeon Creek, he seemed satisfied with producing enough to live from the land, and from occasional earnings as a carpenter. Nat Grigsby said that Tom Lincoln had "few wants and supplied these."[115] Lincoln often worked side-by-side with his father on carpentry projects as well as in the fields. He and his father built an all-wooden wagon, including the wheels, for the Gentry family; they helped to build the Pigeon Creek Meeting House which was used as church; they built the pulpit and the steps for it. And both worked for Josiah and Elizabeth Crawford, who moved to Pigeon Creek in 1824. Abe daubed their cabin and made a split rail fence for them.

The Crawford's moved to Pigeon Creek in 1824. Thomas made all of Elizabeth's furniture. Some thought that Thomas tinkered a lot with his furniture projects but Elizabeth Crawford said that Thomas "was blind in one eye and weak in the other, so he felt his way in the work much of the time: his sense of touch was keen.[116] He was forty-six, and up to this point, he was known as a robust, outdoor and energetic figure.

During his late adolescent years Abe began to yearn for his independence.[117] He often referred to his hired-out work days by saying "I used to be a slave."[118] He seemed to resent giving his father the money he earned, but acquiesced because the law decreed that earnings of sons and daughters until the age of twenty-one went to the father. Not only was it legal, it was a norm of frontier life.

During the years after he left his parents, Lincoln would visit his father and stepmother, and occasionally give them money. He also bought forty acres for them in Coles County in 1841, so that they had the financial security of their home and land.[119] After he married he visited them less often; his wife and children never met his father and stepmother.

Curiously, in 1860, nine years after his father's death, when asked to write a brief autobiographical statement for the 1860 campaign, Lincoln wrote, that his father "grew up literally without education. He never did more in the way of writing than to bunglingly write his own name."[120] For a public statement, this strongly implied criticism of his father. It would have been sufficiently factual and neutral to state that his father had no education. To add the comment about "bunglingly" writing his name served as criticism as well as implying that Lincoln had condescending feelings about his father. One could argue that a loving son would have understood that circumstances did not offer an opportunity for his father, who at the age of eight or nine became a wandering child-laborer in order to survive. Moreover, his father encouraged and paid for his subscription school education.

Their relationship remained ambivalent. In 1850, a year before Abe's father died, Johnston had written to tell him that it appeared that his father was severely ill and dying. Lincoln quickly traveled to see his father and found him to be recovering. A letter informing him that his father was past the crisis arrived after his departure from Springfield.

The following year Johnston wrote Lincoln two letters about Tom's impending death. Lincoln did not respond to these until he received a letter from his niece, Harriet Hanks Chapman, saying that "Father [is very] low and will hardly recover." [121] For Lincoln to make the trip to visit his father, it would have taken three days by horse and buggy from Springfield to Gooseneck Prairie. Johnston in his later years had a history of asking Lincoln for money. Lincoln may have suspected Johnston of "crying wolf" a second time to get Abe to visit and to leave money with them. Lincoln wrote to Johnston that he didn't answer his letters "because it appeared to me I could write nothing which could do any good."

Nevertheless, he wrote affectionately about his father: "You already know I desire that neither father nor mother shall be in want of any comfort, either in health or in sickness, while they live; and I feel sure that you have not failed to use my name, if necessary, to procure a doctor or anything else for father in his present sickness." In the same letter he stated that he could not leave home because his wife was "sick-abed" with a case of "baby-sickness" [after the delivery of a child].[122]

Five days later, when Thomas died on January 17, 1851, Lincoln did not attend the funeral. Nine years later when he visited his grave, he stated that he wanted to place a tombstone on his grave and left instructions about it with Augustus Chapman, grandson of Sarah Lincoln. He never sent Chapman the promised money for a tombstone.[123]

Clearly, he felt closer to his stepmother in his adult years than he did his father.

CHAPTER TWELVE

From the Mind to the Expression to Others: Developing His Oral Persona

Lincoln frequently explained what he had read to his peers. From the age of nine until he was eleven, he lived in a relatively isolated area, because there were few settlements near Pigeon Creek. As he moved into adolescence, there were approximately forty settlements by the time he was thirteen.[124] Not only did this provide sociability for Abe with house raisings, weddings, and special events which included wrestling matches, foot racing games, pitching quoits (iron rings), etc., but it also gave him companions among his peers. "Boys would cluster around him," said Nat Grigsby, "to hear him talk. He made fun and cracked his jokes…but his jokes and fun were at no man's expense." [125]

Through conversation, storytelling, and explanation of what he had read, Abe began a process of testing his understandings from his reading by explaining information and ideas to others. Nat Grigsby said that Lincoln was "figurative in his speeches, talks and conversations;" he argued from "analogy and [he] explained things hard for us to understand by stories, maxims, tales and figures." [126]

Henry Brooner and David Turnham remembered the long horseback rides with Abe to the mill to grind corn and wheat. Abe would hold forth about his readings to them. Able also entertained his peers by his storytelling, gaining practice in what his father had perfected as an art. He told stories to Allen Gentry on their trip to New Orleans and on the return home on a steamship, he engaged passengers in conversation and storytelling.

In his late teens, Gentry's store opened at the crossroads of roads that led to four towns in southern Indiana, Rockport, Bloomington, Corydon, and Boonville. Herndon and Weik cited Gentry's as the "center of wit and wisdom" for those who lived in the area. Lincoln was able to read newspapers there and to engage others in discussions about events, politics, and articles he had read. Again, he entertained people with his storytelling.[127] Abe's stories were from his father and from others such as his blacksmith friend John Baldwin, as well as tales he devised himself. Some saw him as a kind of newsboy; others liked his original and sometimes ridiculous stories. [128]

Lincoln the Preacher

Abe tested his speaking and intellectual skills on his younger stepbrother and sisters. Matilda, his youngest stepsister, remembered that when his stepmother and father went to church "Abe would take down the Bible, read a verse, give out a hymn and we would sing....Abe was about fifteen years of age; he would preach and we would do the crying. Sometimes he would join in the chorus of tears." When Abe attended church he would try to remember the sermon and the way the preacher delivered the Sunday message. Then he would return home and gather children around him, and whoever else was interested, and present what the preacher said that Sunday. Matilda remembered, "Abe would go out to work in the field, get up on a stump and repeat almost word for word the sermon he had heard the Sunday before." [129]

Matilda remembered that Abe also could develop sermons spontaneously. Abe was preaching to children one day when his stepbrother caught a "terrapin" (turtle) and "brought it to the place where Abe was preaching and threw it against the tree [and] crushed the shell and it suffered much, quivered all over. Abe preached against cruelty to animals, contending that an ant's life was to it as sweet as ours to us." Additionally, Matilda remembered that "Often

Abe would make political speeches such as he had heard spoken or seen written....He never forgot anything." [130]

Other Speaking Experiences

Lincoln also gained formal speaking experience through recitation, spelling bees, declamations of prose and poetry, and some debate. Elizabeth Crawford attended some of these school end-of-the-session events. Abe frequently worked for her and had studied her copy of *The Kentucky Preceptor.* "He learned his school orations, speeches, and pieces to recite. Abe attended them, spoke, and acted his part always well, free from rant and swell." [131] Warren claimed that Lincoln "majored in declamation" during his adolescence.[132] He memorized speeches and soliloquies from Scott's *Lessons in Elocution* and Murray's *The English Reader.* [133]

From the ages of seventeen and twenty, Abe would attend trials at the county seat. One lawyer, John Brackenridge, at a murder trial in Boonville, made a strong impression on him. Lincoln complemented him on his clear, logical and powerful presentations. He said it was the "best speech that I, up to that time, ever heard." Years later, as President, Lincoln told Brackenridge that after that trial he "formed a fixed determination to study the law and make that his profession." [134]

On the frontier, Lincoln during his youthful years, especially in Indiana, had discovered two kinds of literacy: (1) the oral literacy that served as the chief communication in the Pigeon Creek community, an orality of storytelling, debating or argumentativeness, spelling bees, pulpit sermonizing, legal disputation in courthouses, and speechmaking; and (2) the discovery through reading printed matter of information, knowledge that became a window to the literate world which influenced and governed the affairs of western hemispheric society through prose, poetry, drama, essays, and legal documents.

CHAPTER THIRTEEN

From the Mind to Expression to Others: Developing His Written Persona

Clearly, Abe Lincoln loved the written word as much as he loved the spoken word. Once he learned to put letters together, he began to maintain a copybook of words, quotations and key excerpts from his spelling and elocution books that he wanted to memorize or ponder. Lincoln told John Scripps who interviewed him to compose a campaign biography in 1859, that as a young boy he wrote "letters…words…wherever he found suitable material. He scrawled them with charcoal…scored them in the dust, in the sand, in the snow – anywhere and everywhere that lines could be drawn, there he improved his capacity for writing." [135]

The first letter he wrote was borne out of grief for his mother. Abe wrote a letter to Rev. David Elkin their former pastor of the Little Mount Church in Kentucky. Abe asked him to come to Pigeon Creek and conduct a service at his mother's grave.[136] Elkin came to Pigeon Creek during the following year and conducted a graveside service for Nancy Lincoln, and then visited his son who was living in Indiana.

For eleven years Abe acted as a scribe for his neighbors in Indiana. While living in New Salem, Abe told Mentor Graham, a friend and tutor to him, that he came to understand other people's thoughts and feelings by learning to put their sentiments into written language.[137]

Journalistic Essays

Lincoln's first known essay was about the wickedness of cruelty to animals; he wrote this essay while in school. He had begun writing sentences on the subject; then, he developed an essay, an assignment not taught in the subscription schools. "Abe took it up on his own accord," said Nathaniel Grigsby, a school friend and neighbor.[138] Sometime during 1826 or 1827, when Lincoln was about eighteen years old, he read an 1826 newspaper given to him by John Romine. The newspaper featured articles about the fiftieth anniversary of the United States, an editorial on Thomas Jefferson's death as well as reports of the coincidental deaths of John Adams and Jefferson, both dying on July 4, 1826. They were the only two patriots among the signers of the Declaration of Independence who became President.[139]

Subsequently, Abe wrote an essay on the United States government. He extolled the virtues of the American government, said the US Constitution "was the best form of government for an intelligent people," and should be held "sacred" and the "Union perpetuated, and its laws revered and enforced." William Wood, a neighbor and friend to Abe, read the essay and showed it to a lawyer, John Pitcher, who found Abe's sentiments the best he had read. Pitcher reportedly said, "The world can't beat it," and he had it published in a newspaper.[140] Abe had also written an essay on temperance that Wood showed to a local minister, Rev. Aaron Farmer. Farmer liked the essay so much that he sent it to a temperance newspaper in Ohio for publication.[141] Wood saw printed copies of both essays, but none of Lincoln's essays from this period have survived. Neither are his notes on these subjects that may have appeared in one of his copybooks extant. What remain of his notes are largely arithmetic problems and exercises and a few rhymes.

Among the rhymes extant in his copybook is one that is closer to poetry than verse or doggerel. It is preceded by the line "Abraham Lincoln his hand and pen / He will be good but god knows when" followed by eight lines about the fleetingness of time in his handwriting, without punctuation or the visual form of poetry. These eight lines have erroneously been attributed to Lincoln as his original work. Herndon and Weik and Basler had cited it thusly. Wilson and Davis discovered that Lincoln had copied the verse of a hymn he evidently liked on the fleetingness of time. This verse is from a hymn by Isaac Watts, *Hymns and Spirituals,* published in 1707, "The Shortness of Life and The Goodness of God," Book II.[142]

During Lincoln's late teen years, he wrote a number of crude and satirical verses. The most remembered one is "The Chronicles of Reuben," a biting, satirical piece written in biblical style. The original complete text did not survive, but several settlers in the Pigeon Creek area remembered parts of the satirical verse "better than the Bible." [143] The verse is known by what Elizabeth Crawford and others remember, thirty-six years later, as recited to Herndon.[144]

The death of his sister, Sarah Lincoln Grigsby, became the reason Lincoln wrote this piece. Married in 1826 to Aaron Grigsby, she died in childbirth in 1828. Lincoln and his family felt that the Grigsbys waited too long into her laboring period before contacting a doctor, and they believed that it caused her death. The Grigsbys countered by saying that by the time he arrived, the doctor was too drunk to be able to save her life.[145]

The Grigsbys were considered prosperous in the Pigeon Creek community. They had a large two-story log cabin home and they raised ten children. When the Grigsbys celebrated the marriages of two of their sons, Charles and Reuben, who married on the same day, they did not invite the Lincolns to the celebration dinner, or infare, as it was known then.

Abe clearly wrote this satire on the Grigsby family as a consequence of the exclusion of his family. The piece revolves around the custom of preparing the bedrooms for the two couples, and ending the celebration by escorting the grooms to their bedrooms where their respective brides awaited them, in this case, the wrong bridegrooms for the wrong brides.

There is some understanding that Lincoln himself engineered the joke on the newlyweds by making the waiters confederates in the joke. The waiters evidently were the ones who escorted the grooms to the wrong rooms. One of the brides, Betsy Grigsby, denied that the joke ever happened: "Lincoln just wrote that for mischief."[146]

It is not clear if Abe, in fact, did actually stage the mix-up. What does seem clear is that Abe generated the story of a bridal mix-up in verse, a few months after the weddings in 1829. He left it in a strategic place for a member of the Grigsby family to find. Although the author was "unknown," it was clear to the settlers that this was a typical Abe Lincoln piece. First, he was more literate than anyone in the community among the young people; second, he was known for his storytelling and his verse on special occasions; and third, he was also known as a prankster. Additionally, he knew the Bible and clearly could draw upon it, i.e., farcically extending the biblical Book of Chronicles with the "Chronicles of Reuben," implying, because of the number of Grigsbys, that there were more chapters to come. Artfully, he developed a "biblical" tone by using well-known phrases such as "Now there was a man who...." and "It came to pass...."etc.

While in this satirical mood, Lincoln included a commentary about Josiah Crawford, who made him pick corn blades for two days to pay for Weems' book on Washington. Crawford, known for the length of his nose and sometimes referred to as "old blue nose," became "...Josiah, blowing his bugle and making sound so great the neighboring hills and valleys echoed with resounding acclamation." Lincoln had the waiters at the feast taking the brides to their bedrooms first, and then escorting the grooms to the wrong brides. The mother, Mrs. Grigsby, discovered the error and rousted her sons, perhaps before it was too late, and they, in haste to get to the right bedroom, bumped into each other.

The one verse that many remembered is bawdy and gross. This was an added stanza about William Grigsby, referred to as Billy.

> For Reuben and Charles have married two girls,
> But Billy has married a boy.
> The girls he had tried on every side,
> But none could he get to agree;
>
> All was in vain, he went home again,
> And since then he's married to Natty.
> So Billy and Natty agreed very well,
> And momma's well pleased with the match.
>
> The egg is laid, but Natty's afraid
> The shell is too soft it never will hatch,
> But Betsy, she said, "You cursed bald head,
> My suitor you never can be,
>
> Besides your low crotch proclaims you a botch
> And that can never answer for me."

William challenged Lincoln to a fight over this, but Lincoln said he was too big and strong to fight him on an equal level. His stepbrother, John substituted for Abe. The fight became brutal enough so that Abe had to pull them apart and stop it. John sustained some serious injuries for a time from this fight.[147]

Later in life, Lincoln became quite adept at satirizing his opponents on the campaign circuit. On the stump it was one of his best stratagems. In the Pigeon Creek-Gentryville area, "The Chronicles of Reuben" became part of the folklore for awhile. Nathaniel Grigsby, years later, said, "The satire was good—sharp—cutting and showed the genius of the boy; it hurt us then, but it's all over now."[148]

CHAPTER FOURTEEN

Reading Becomes Lincoln's Window to the World at Twenty-One

At the age of twenty-one, Abraham Lincoln had developed key heroes and role models of leadership of democratic statesmanship and ideals. He preferred the idyllic depiction of George Washington as a gentlemanly leader and statesman who urged rationalism and moderation. In Benjamin Franklin, he found that his "up from the bootstraps" life resonated with his frontier circumstances and rural poverty. Franklin's life also informed Lincoln that he could make any life-choice he wished, and he could attain it, as did Franklin, through hard work and mental discipline to overcome hardships.

Lincoln drew much of his political thought from Henry Clay. Clay inspired him for the soundness of his ideas about the direction the United States should take: a national system of internal improvements of roads and waterways that would help the states economically; a protective tariff that would encourage greater distribution of the wealth, and the gradual emancipation of the slaves. Years later, as a politician, Lincoln would cite Clay as a teacher and leader, his "beau ideal of a statesman." [149]

Further support for Lincoln's ideology of the United States could have come from Lincoln's reading of William Grimshaw's *A History of the United States from Their First Settlement to the Cession of Florida in Eighteen Hundred and Twenty-One.* Grimshaw was one of the few American historians in the early eighteen hundreds. According to Lincoln's stepsister Matilda Johnston Moore, this was the one history book he had read.[150]   Otherwise he came to understand the history of the United States through its fundamental documents, *The Declaration of Independence,* and *The Constitution,* and what he could learn from political biographies.

Grimshaw wrote from a moral point of view about the fledgling democracy.   While lauding the new experiment in freedom and human progress, he also emphasized that the young nation needed to correct two major sins: one was the usurpation of the land from Native Americans, and the other was the practice of slavery which began, ironically, with the extension of a freer, more popular government in Jamestown, Virginia, 1620.   In order to make true progress, Grimshaw advocated that the United States needed to treat Native-Americans better and it needed to end slavery.[151]

Two Major Books of Learning: *Lessons in Elocution* and *The English Reader*

Lincoln encountered other ideas as well as a wider sense of the human condition from two influential books that he read and reread: William Scott's *Elements of Elocution,* and Lindley Murray's *The English Reader.*   Fred Kaplan in *Lincoln The Biography of a Writer,* cited these two books, both available to Lincoln during his adolescent years, as seminal influences in presenting a wide range of classical and British thought.   Kaplan believed that these books provided an "intellectual groundwork on which to advance his [Lincoln's] cautious and reasoning temperament." [152]

Sarah Bush Lincoln is believed to have brought William Scott's *Lessons in Elocution,* with her when she married Tom Lincoln in 1819. Her edition was bought in 1806.[153]   Lincoln also studied from another edition that his friend David Turnham owned, published in 1779.[154]

Lessons in Elocution

Like Murray's *The English Reader,* Scott's *Lessons...* included a wide range of literary selections from classical literature of the Greek and Roman period, as well as speeches, articles, essays, and poetry mainly from English writers. Both books enjoyed a century of influence in American education during the nineteenth and early twentieth centuries.

Other than an occasional quotation, *Lessons in Elocution* became Lincoln's first introduction to Shakespeare. In the 1820 edition, Scott included twenty-one soliloquies. Lincoln learned about the emotional turmoil of characters such as Hamlet who was duty-bound to avenge his father's murder, who felt ambivalent about his mother for her hasty marriage to his uncle, and, at the same time, considered his own death: "To be or not to be / that is the question." Scott also included Claudius' soliloquy when he admits to murdering Hamlet's father.

There are soliloquies from Henry IV and V, by Hotspur, Henry and Falstaff (Falstaff's arrogant dismissal of honor as meaningless); Othello's loving speech on how he came to marry his wife, Desdemona; three soliloquies from Julius Caesar, by Cassius to Brutus, and Brutus' speech to the Romans, and the famous oration by Marc Antony over the dead body of Caesar. Lincoln learned about Shakespeare's world, that human actions cause major upsets that imbalance the world, that unhealthy love, guilt, jealousy, and lust for power wreak havoc beyond measure in the lives of people. One of the final soliloquies is Jacques' speech on the ages of man: from *As You Like It*: "All the world is a stage / And all the men and women merely players." Its melancholy theme might have resonated with Lincoln, i.e., Jacque's outline of the stages of life to the end, "Sans teeth, sans life, sans everything."

Lessons also included possible influences on Abe with speeches by Cicero and Cato. Also prominent in *Lessons* were Hugh Blair's lectures and sermons on piety to God, on benevolence and humanity, as well as excerpts on Public Speaking, and on the true patriot. David Hume's "The Advance of History" and Addison's response to "Cato: on The Immortality of the Soul" from *The Spectator* were also featured in *Lessons*.

The English Reader

Lincoln told William Herndon that he regarded Murray's *The English Reader,* as the best schoolbook ever put in the hands of an American youth.[155] Like Scott and other authors of the day, Murray emphasized that his selection of material was based on moral principles necessary to develop young minds. At best, the book is a selective range of classical and English literature, drawing on the thinkers and writers of these periods of human history, including biographical profiles, articles from *Spectator,* by Addison and Steele, speeches by Cicero, the Apostle Paul, Hugh Blair, Lord Mansfield, etc.

Kaplan suggested that Lincoln read ideas from *The English Reader* that reinforced his evolving ideas about democracy, rationalism, and government. Many of the readings feature writing by proponents of the enlightenment, advocates who advanced the notion of scientific inquiry through the use of reason and evidence. Thus, John Locke in a dialogue with Pierre Bayle, questioned judgments made on the basis of intuition and irrational thought, and argued that religious inquiry should be based on an enlightenment standard: "True religion values reason and evidence rather than irrational enthusiasm." Advocating for tolerance of new ideas, Locke urged wide-ranging inquiry as a method for advancing human development and progress (Dialogues: 140-146, 1826 ed). In a true spirit of enlightenment, Lord Mansfield arguing in Parliament against a bill that would delay justice for its members accused of a crime while they were sitting in Parliament, articulated a standard of justice: "True liberty...can only exist when justice is equally administered to all; to the king and to the beggar." (pp. 156-160, 1826 edition).

Kaplan made connections between Lincoln's reading and other enlightened thinkers such as Pope's affirmation of a higher power, the "Father of All!" who maintains order, reason and equity. According to Kaplan, this would be compatible with Lincoln's thinking about religion that would lead him ultimately to accept the notion of harmony among Christian ethics, classical style, and natural law.[156]

The English Reader includes an abundance of Bishop Hugh Blair's sermons and lectures on moral philosophy. Blair opposed Calvinistic doctrines of original sin ("In Adam's fall we sinned all.") that led to man's corruption and ultimate damnation. He addressed moral questions more than theological ones. He had studied Locke's famous essay, "On Human Understanding." A few years later when he lived in New Salem, Lincoln studied Hugh Blair's *Rhetoric and Belles Lettres,* a synthesis of rhetorical theory for public discourse and the study of literary criticism, under the tutelage of Mentor Graham.

Kaplan also stated that Lincoln's tendency toward melancholy drew him to Thomas Gray's poetry, especially "Elegy Written in a Country Churchyard." which he had memorized. Lincoln could identify with Gray's exposition of hard working country laborers, who, although talented or ambitious, could not overcome their lowly station in life. Interestingly, when Lincoln was asked to describe his early life, he summarized it with one line from Gray's *"Elegy..."*: "the simple annuals of the poor." Lincoln also enjoyed memorizing Oliver Wendell Holmes poetry in his adult life, especially "The Last Leaf" which expressed sadness about the fleetingness of time. Kaplan noted a goodness of fit between Lincoln and Holmes' melancholy and humorous poetry; those were two prominent personality traits of Lincoln.[157]

Replica of the Berry-Lincoln Store
Lincoln's New Salem Historic Site, Illinois

CHAPTER FIFTEEN

Transferring Self-Learning to Illinois: The Final Influence

New Salem, Illinois: The Frontier Town that Launched Abraham Lincoln

For the first time in his life, at the age of twenty-two, Abe was completely on his own. He moved to New Salem, a log-cabin commercial town established near the Sangamon River in 1829, to service settlers in the outlying Illinois territory. Abe described himself at this time as a "piece of floating driftwood."

New Salem, in its brief existence of fifteen years, included four general stores, two doctors, a shoemaker, carpenter, and teacher, as well as a tavern and wool-carding mill. An estimated twenty-five families lived in New Salem. [158]

During his seven years in New Salem, 1831-1837, Lincoln flourished as much as the town. He found new occupations for his abilities, and he was able to refine his education, his speaking effectiveness, and to expand his general studies. Essentially New Salem offered him a transitional and nurturing environment that led to his career as a lawyer and politician.

Abe found work in New Salem as a rail-splitter and odd jobs man, as a store clerk and proprietor, election clerk, postmaster, and land surveyor. He learned about New Salem in the late spring of 1831. He and his cousin John Hanks and stepbrother John Johnston, were hired by Denton Offutt to build a flatboat and deliver Offutt's goods to be sold in New Orleans. The flatboat ran aground at Rutledge's milldam on the Sangamon River at New Salem. The spring runoff had subsided and the dammed water caused the New Salem section to become quite shallow. "We landed at the New Salem mill…and got fast on Rutledge's mill dam," recalled John Hanks.[159]

A number of townspeople observed this event. They saw a tall, dark-haired Abe Lincoln in jeans cloth wading in the water trying to find a way to dislodge the boat and save the goods onboard. The front of the flatboat was pointed upward while the rear of the boat began to take on water.[160]

Mentor Graham, the town's schoolteacher, recognized Lincoln. His family knew the Lincolns in Kentucky. Mentor borrowed an auger so that Lincoln could bore a hole in the boat to let the water out. Before that, however, they unloaded the goods onto a borrowed boat from one of the townspeople.[161]

Once the boat was released and the goods reloaded on the flatboat, the crew proceeded down the Sangamon to meet the Illinois River and ultimately connect with the Mississippi River to New Orleans. Once again on this his second trip to New Orleans, Lincoln saw slaves being auctioned, and according to John Hanks, "It ran like iron into him."[162]

After the New Orleans trip, Denton Offutt, offered Lincoln a job in a store he established in New Salem. Lincoln's duties included clerking and basically running the store as well as tending to a huge amount of corn for a large herd of hogs that Offutt brought to New Salem. His first task was to build a split-rail fence for the hogs.

As Lincoln established himself in New Salem, he demonstrated that he was an amiable person given to telling anecdotes and stories, as well as enjoying conversations with others. Mentor Graham noted that Lincoln was unfailingly courteous and respectful of customers and this engendered a sense of good will.[163]

Within a month, Lincoln became one of the election clerks. Mentor Graham knew Lincoln had writing skills and evidently recommended him. Lincoln was sworn into the job and this became his first public office.[164]

Lincoln also became known for his physical strength, and it wasn't long before he was asked to demonstrate this. Offutt boasted of Abe's physical prowess, and Jack Armstrong and his Clary Grove gang challenged Lincoln to a wrestling match. Armstrong, also known for his physical strength, and his cohorts were generally known as ruffians who had a kind of protectiveness about New Salem.

The match was prolonged, as both men seemed to be of equal strength. Armstrong tried to call a "Foul," and Lincoln was upset with this stratagem and caught him by the throat and held him at arm's length. Armstrong's friends saw that he was at a disadvantage and started to join the match against Lincoln. Abe told them he would wrestle each one in turn but not all of them at once. They backed off and evidently the match ended in a draw, although there are different versions with some indication that Lincoln had won the match.[165] Regardless, after the contest Lincoln gained acceptance, and he and Armstrong became good friends.

Lincoln resumed his practice of writing documents for people as he had in Indiana, without charge.[166] *Lincoln, Day By Day* chronicles a number of legal statements, deeds, loans, and contracts that Lincoln wrote for people in New Salem, during 1832-35.[167]

Six months after he arrived in New Salem, Lincoln filed his candidacy for representative to the Illinois legislature. Offutt's store had become a failing venture. The Black Hawk war erupted in Illinois, and Lincoln, along with other young men in the New Salem area including some of the Clary Grove gang, enlisted as privates. Within a day or two he was elected as their Captain. He served for four months, and earned a reputation as a fair-minded leader who looked after the needs of his men.[168] Upon his discharge from the army Lincoln resumed his campaigning. He was defeated, running eighth in a field of candidates, but encouraged by the number of votes he received from New Salem, 277 of 300. [169]

Lincoln began to connect with the legal world once again when he found a copy of Blackstone's *Commentaries on English Law* at the bottom of a barrel of rubbish. As Lincoln told the story, a man migrating westward stopped by his store and asked him to buy an old barrel for which he had no room in his wagon. Lincoln bought it for fifty cents, put the barrel aside and forgot about it. While reorganizing the goods in the store, he rediscovered the barrel, emptied out its contents and found a copy of Blackstone's book. He said, "The more I read the more intensely interested I became. Never in my whole life was my mind so thoroughly absorbed." [170]

During his first year in New Salem, Lincoln also developed intellectual friends, notably Mentor Graham, the schoolteacher, and Bowling Green, lawyer and Justice of the Peace. Green believed that "there was good material" in Lincoln and that "he only wanted education."[171] Green became a kind of surrogate father to Lincoln. Green was Mentor Graham's first friend in New Salem and Graham introduced Abe to him. Lincoln traded newspapers and books with Graham and Bowling Green. Green, known as a cultured man who had refined manners, was also a figure of stability in New Salem. He maintained order and frequently arbitrated disputes among farmers and tradesmen, and put drunks in jail.

Green, Graham and Lincoln often spent evenings discussing ideas, or, a favorite topic like the kind of progress required to make New Salem a strong community. Graham was especially persistent on temperance; Green and Lincoln were liked–minded but not quite as intense as the schoolmaster, who eventually joined the temperance movement and was expelled by his Baptist church because he joined a "movement." [172]

William Mentor Graham was encouraged by his father, Jeremiah, from a very young age to become a schoolteacher. Jeremiah had relatives who were educated and he saw the advantages for his red-haired son who was born with a hearing loss in one ear. Mentor was also taught all the rudiments of running a farm, hunting for food, and other basic frontier tasks by his father.

He was also encouraged to learn reading, writing and arithmetic, not only from subscription schools but also from a two-year sojourn with his uncle, Robert Graham. Robert Graham was an itinerant doctor for rural people who owned a sizable library of books. Mentor accompanied him on his trips and Robert Graham tutored him daily. Whether at home or on the road Mentor was responsible for completing a lesson and reciting it to him. When Mentor returned to his parents, he also attended Nathaniel Owens Bush Creek Academy at a nearby plantation for several months.

Afterward, he collected books when he had "pay-work"; his father allowed him to keep some of his earned money. Mentor continued studying, maintaining a self-teaching practice for the rest of his life.[173]

As a teacher, Mentor was a strict taskmaster who kept his students busy and responsible for their lessons. He spent his evenings copying material from books for his students. He ran skill-drilling sessions with his students in addition to their daily recitations. During the school day when he recognized that the children were getting tired, he would read them a story.[174] He also gave the younger children walking to school a ride on his horse. Mentor taught school, maintained his farm and also developed a brick making business.

Mentor and Abe were kindred spirits. They admired Henry Clay and his political positions; they were pro-temperance and anti-slavery; they liked to hear legal cases tried in courts; and they loved reading. At some point during his first year, Lincoln said to Mentor, "I had a notion to study grammar," and Mentor replied that if he wanted any public position, studying grammar would be the "best thing he could do." [175]

Abe lived six months with Mentor Graham, his wife and family, spending many evenings reciting from Kirkham's *Grammar, i.e.* Samuel Kirkham, *English Grammar In Familiar Lectures, Accompanied by a Compendium; Embracing a New Systematick Order of Parsing, A New System of Punctuation.* The book included parts of speech, diagramming or parsing, punctuation and its theory. It had a section on prosody, i.e., forms of poetry, accents and meters; a section on rhetoric, i.e., sentences of various kinds for various uses, and eloquent word order. "Good Writing" was another unique chapter. Kirkham also offered bits of advice to the student. For example: "Do not commit and rehearse this book. Read one or two sentences, then look off the book and repeat their contents in *your* words, [and] in your mind." [176]

Graham helped his older students, including Lincoln, to improve their speaking ability. Students were asked to speak their own ideas or the words of some great mind, excerpted from a book. He would correct pronunciations and discourage colloquial speech, such as "It cain't never," or, in Lincoln's case, his Indiana frontier localisms. Students were asked to repeat their recitations or speeches until they could do it without the intrusion of colloquial speech. [177]

Graham also set a goal with Lincoln to connect his learning. Lincoln, he stated, "knew many things well, but not their interrelation." He wanted to make Lincoln's education "a clean, straight line." [178] Consequently, Lincoln not only studied grammar with Mentor, but also arithmetic, philosophy, astronomy, and literature.[179] Graham had a fine collection of English literature and selected translations of classical writings.[180] Graham noted that Lincoln had no training in "geometry and trigonometry." [181] He introduced Lincoln to these principles, but he also introduced Lincoln to John Calhoun, the county surveyor. Graham knew that Calhoun was looking for able men to help survey the new lands in the county. Calhoun gave Lincoln time to learn surveying. Lincoln, assisted by Mentor Graham, studied a book by Flint and Gibson on surveying.[182]

Within six weeks Lincoln had mastered Flint's practical discussion on surveying and Gibson's treatise on geometry and trigonometry. He started with the northwest section of Sangamon county, learning to lay out routes for roads and land parcels. He still relied on Graham's help. First, he would measure the land, its distances, corners, and directions. Then, as Graham's daughter Elizabeth remembered, "He would call at our house and get my father to calculate the figures." They would often "sit till midnight calculating." [183]

During this period, Lincoln worked as a part-time Postmaster as well as a surveyor. He had debts to pay, financial notes that he and William Berry, his business partner had signed when they began their store. A few years later, Berry, who had a severe drinking problem, died. Lincoln inherited that debt as well. When he could, Lincoln sent money to his father and stepmother. As late as 1848, Lincoln was still paying off the debt that he had accrued from his New Salem business ventures.[184]

A debate club had been formed in New Salem with James Rutledge, the co-founder of New Salem as its President. Mentor Graham and Bowling Green were members, and Mentor invited Abe to attend. Robert Rutledge, tells the story of Lincoln's first speaking appearance addressing the group on an issue. The assembly smiled when Lincoln arose to speak, "for all anticipated the relation of some humorous story. But he opened up the discussion in splendid style to the infinite astonishment of his friends.... He pursued the question with reason and argument so pithy and forcible that all were amazed." [185] James Rutledge told his wife that "there was more in Abe's head than wit and fun, that he was already a fine speaker, that all he lacked was culture to enable him to reach a high destiny." Shortly after this speech, James Rutledge encouraged Abe to run for the state legislature. So debating, as well as speeches, recitations, and discussion of ideas were part of Lincoln's intense study, preparation, and experiences during this period.

Sculpture of Abraham Lincoln as a surveyor
by John McClarey
A gift from the Illinois Professional Land Surveyors Assoc.
Displayed at Lincoln's New Salem Historic Site, Illinois

CHAPTER SIXTEEN

Love and Death:
Lincoln and Ann Rutledge

Many of the older students studied with Mentor Graham at his home, around his gate-legged table, and that included Ann Rutledge and Abe Lincoln. They shared the *Grammar* book. Abe would walk her home late in the evening, and the two developed a close relationship. They considered themselves engaged and they expected to be married once Abe earned his law license.[186] Ann had been previously engaged to James McNeil who had come to New Salem to make his fortune, and who operated a store with Sam Hill. He had left his Ohio home clandestinely after his family lost most of their wealth. He took an assumed name so that his family would not find him. He wanted to make his fortune so that he could return to his family and remedy their loss of wealth. In the meantime, he had become engaged to Ann Rutledge. Then, he left New Salem to see his family and learned that his father had died. Evidently the circumstances of the family were such that required him to remain and help. His real name was McNamar, not McNeil.[187] Ann did not hear from him after he left New Salem. Because of his lengthy absence and his silence, she had decided that the marriage was not going to happen. She confided this to Arminda Rogers, a confidant and a tutor to Ann of Blair's *Rhetoric and Belle Lettres* and Kirkham's *Grammar.*[188]

At that point Lincoln stepped in and pursued her. Ann was preparing to enter the Jacksonville Academy for Women, and she was one of Mentor's advanced learners improving her grammar, writing skills, understanding of ideas, philosophy, Latin, etc. in anticipation of the curriculum at the academy. She clearly told her brother Robert that she and Abe planned to marry, but that she wanted to inform McNamar of the change in her feelings and "seek an honorable release." [189]

Ann Rutledge, considered a beautiful woman, was seventeen when she and Lincoln became enamored of each other. Robert said she was the brightest of all the children in their family. Then in 1835, several members of the Rutledge family were ill from a malarial or typhoid fever that was raging among the New Salem townspeople. Lincoln and his friend Dr. John Allen spent several days caring for them. Lincoln, Graham and others made coffins to bury the dead. [190] Ann Rutledge was the last of her family to contract the illness and she was unable to overcome it. After five days, she died August 25, 1835.

I have "Nothing to live for Graham. I feel like taking my own life..." - Abe to Mentor Graham [191]

Lincoln was so devastated with grief that a number of his friends thought he was losing his reason. He talked of committing suicide, and they began a watch on him. [192] He contracted the illness, too, and Dr. Allen asked the Bowling Greens if they would take care of him. He wanted to remove Lincoln from the sickness so that he could regain his health and be with people who might help him with his grief. [193] Lincoln was with them for three weeks. Dr. Allen visited him, and Mrs. Green ministered to his needs. The day-to-day contact with Bowling Green and his wife helped Lincoln to overcome his initial despair, but it was a long time before people could say he was no longer melancholy. [194] He could not bear, he told friends, that there should be rain and snow and storms over Ann's grave. [195] For the first time in his life, he had experienced a deep love relationship and a sense of commitment to a woman. Later he said any woman he loved in the future would surely die, like his mother, his sister, and Ann Rutledge. [196]

CHAPTER SEVENTEEN

Three Mentors: BowlingGreen, Jack Kelso and Mentor Graham

Bowling Green and Lincoln

Lincoln borrowed law books from Bowling Green and he enjoyed attending Green's Justice of the Peace court. Green appreciated his witticisms in court as well as his observations. Eventually he made Abe the "next friend" in the court, a kind of paralegal. Frequently, he wrote legal forms, deeds, wills, contracts, and agreements that emerged from court appearances before Bowling Green. Mentor Graham had given Lincoln a book of legal forms. In the absence of lawyers in New Salem Lincoln often assumed that position for the plaintiff or the defendant. Once, he was asked to assume a lawyer's position in Concord for Squire Berry. He represented the case of an unmarried mother. Lincoln argued through metaphor. A man's character, he noted, was like a white cloth, which though soiled could become clean again through washing and hanging it in the sun to dry. An unmarried mother's character, however, was probably less to blame than the man, because she was like a broken and shattered bottle or glass vase that could never be made whole again. Lincoln did not charge any fees for his work for Bowling Green's court, but it served as a paralegal apprenticeship for him.[197]

Throughout his development as a young adult, Lincoln never failed to impress others with his abilities. They in turn saw potential in him and helped him as they could. Everyone who had a book or newspaper willingly loaned it to him to read, both during his Indiana years and in New Salem.

Jack Kelso

In New Salem, there were other friends who helped Lincoln such as John (Jack) Kelso, an educated frontiersman living in New Salem. He was considered an expert hunter and fisherman. He also sold smoked reindeer hams in New Salem.[198] But he was known for his outstanding knowledge of the poetry of Robert Burns and his knowledge of Shakespeare's plays. He introduced Burns' poetry to Abe who became a lover of his poetry from that time on.[199] He and Kelso would trade their memorizations of various poems and passages from these two great writers. And they liked to argue the issues of the day.[200]

James Short and William Greene trust Lincoln

James Short, a good friend to Abe since he first arrived in New Salem, bought Abe's horse, saddle and surveying equipment when it was seized as part payment for debts owed by Lincoln and Berry. William Greene had signed the original note to Lincoln and Berry. Short knew that Lincoln would need the horse and equipment to make a living (the post office had closed after two years), so he gave them back to Lincoln.[201] Greene paid the remainder of what was owed on the note. Abe eventually repaid Short and Greene.[202]

One of the long-term outcomes of Lincoln's study of geometry and his work in surveying was his interest in Euclid's *Geometry*. After he embarked on his career as a lawyer and politician, Lincoln continued to study the book and kept it with him as he traveled two or three times a year as a circuit lawyer in Illinois. Both John T. Stuart and Judge David Davis noted that Abe carried the book with him and studied from it during his evenings on the circuit from 1846 to 1855.[203]

Abe must have liked the challenge of the logical deductive process Euclid developed beginning with a set of axioms and then proving the propositions or theorems from those axioms. The second section of the book contained number theory with numbers treated geometrically by way of representing segments of various lengths. Finally, the book presented axioms about solid geometry, its dimensions and ratios. Evidently, for Lincoln, the challenge was always there to be mastered. It is not known if he completed his study of the book.

A Town Named for Lincoln

Lincoln's surveying experience combined with his legal work also led to another outcome. A town in Illinois was named after him. He had worked in the area, generally known as Postville, for several years as a circuit lawyer. In 1853, as a legal representative for the railroad; Abe was instrumental in identifying that the railroad should stop for fuel and water at Postville in Logan County, thus increasing that region's commercial viability. Lincoln also helped to plot the street layout of the town. So, the townspeople decided to rename the town as Lincoln, Illinois. It was the first town to be named for him before he became President.[204]

Mentor Graham: Lincoln and New Salem

Finally, the one person who steadfastly helped Lincoln to focus on his future career, and who followed his activities after he left New Salem was Mentor Graham. Mentor attended circuit courts from time to time to hear Lincoln argue and present his cases. He attended some of the Lincoln–Douglas debates. On his inauguration Mentor sat in the first row so that he could hear Lincoln's address as President in 1861. Lincoln saw Mentor in the first row and invited him to sit on the platform. Mentor was escorted to the platform and sat with all the other dignitaries: a fitting acknowledgement of Mentor's contribution.[205]

The town of New Salem began to diminish by 1840 as the promise of commercial traffic and commerce by steamboat on the Sangamon River failed to become a reality. But New Salem and young Abraham Lincoln were good for each other. Its townspeople came to know Lincoln's quality and potential, and many of its citizens encouraged and nurtured the homespun frontiersman from Indiana. Lincoln, with self-studying ingrained in his persona, benefited from their help, their resourcefulness and their faith in him. It was and still remains, a remarkable relationship.

Replica of the combined cabin of Jack Kelso- and Joshua Miller
The Kelso family occupied the left side.
The Miller family occupied the right side.
Lincoln's New Salem Historic Site, Illinois

CHAPTER EIGHTEEN

Governance and Lincoln: His Experiences from Pigeon Creek to New Salem

Pigeon Creek

At a basic level, during his Indiana boyhood, Lincoln experienced and learned how governance and its structures are developed. In Pigeon Creek, slowly as the need arose, settlers recognized the mutuality of their needs in that environment. They began to establish their ways of living, i.e., governance and social norms. Respect for property rights, the need for right conduct to prevail throughout the settlement, and a system of justice as outlined by Constitutional rights, were basic to their existence, especially as more settlers came into the region. Established settlers helping with house raisings for new families was a basic norm of good will and a sign of mutual cooperativeness. The establishment of a building in Pigeon Creek by community effort, that could serve as a school and as a church was a key development. These were two institutions in a society that generated ethical systems. In part this demonstrated the influence of the Bible, the moral teachings of the frontier parents, and the adherence to known laws from settlers' other living experiences. Throughout his fourteen years in Indiana, Abe grew up with the gradual implementation of a government for Pigeon Creek and for Spencer County, in effect, the establishment of a community in a larger democracy.

New Salem Launched Lincoln's Career in Politics

In New Salem, the commercial village of tradesmen was ripe with grass-roots democracy. Its basic governmental processes had been newly established when Abe arrived. There was also a prevailing sense of equality among its citizens, a sense of shared power with equal opportunity to participate in government. There were few economic or other contrasts among the settlers. Anyone wanting to run for office could. The opportunities available within the political landscape of New Salem and Sangamon County were perfect for the next layer of Lincoln's education and development.

At twenty-three, Lincoln had inherited his father's robust health and had followed his verbal example; his mother encouraged him to read and write; both parents emphasized the moral teachings from the Bible. Sarah Bush Lincoln nurtured his self-study habits, and his individuality. Josiah and Elizabeth Crawford, William Wood, David Turnham, and James Gentry gave him books and periodicals to read, thus, validating his self-study abilities. His informal and formal mentorships from Bowling Green, Mentor Graham, James Rutledge, and John Kelso in New Salem, helped him to expand his knowledge and skills, and to focus his ambition toward the study of law and to enter political life.

Abraham Lincoln studying while riding on the prairie
by Ann Hyat Huntington
Lincoln's New Salem Historic Site, Illinois

PART THREE

Lincoln Presents Himself
To The Public

My fellow citizens. I have been solicited by many friends to become a candidate for the legislature. I have so concluded to do so. I presume you all know who I am. My name is Abraham Lincoln. My politics is short and sweet like an old woman's dance. I am in favor of a national bank, high and protective tariff and the internal improvement system.

If elected I will be thankful. If beaten I can do as I have been doing and work for a living.

This was an impromptu speech Lincoln delivered at Papasville, Illinois. He was the only candidate in attendance at a large gathering of people attending a sale.

-Speech was recollected by James A. Herndon, in 1865, in a letter to William H. Herndon, *HI*, May 29m 1865,pp. 16-17. This was Lincoln's second campaign (1834) for legislative office.

CHAPTER NINETEEN

Lincoln Becomes a Politician

Shortly after Lincoln participated in his first debate, James Rutledge, co-founder of New Salem, urged Lincoln to run for the legislature.[206] Thus, after living six months in New Salem, Lincoln announced his candidacy for office with his "Communication to the People of Sangamo County," the *Sangamo Journal,* March 9, 1832.[207]

He and Mentor Graham worked diligently to craft a political statement of a young man perceptive about Sangamon County and its needs. They argued about each position he should take, and then refined the wording of each phrase of the document.[208] Much of the formal statements of introduction and transitional paragraphs could be attributed to Mentor Graham because of his familiarity with election documents. The analysis of internal improvements and its specificity could easily be Lincoln's own. The two also consulted with John McNamar, (then known by the alias of McNeil), who lived in New Salem at that time and who had a college education. He made some grammatical suggestions to the document.[209]

Seven paragraphs specifically dealt with internal improvements, mainly to widen the Sangamon river in the thirty-five mile area before Beardstown as the most expedient means of creating greater access to markets. One paragraph stated that usury laws needed to be fairer on interest rates and the practice of jailing the debtor needed to end, a supportive statement of President Jackson's message to Congress in 1831. Another paragraph focused on education and advocated greater universality of basic education for all citizens because this would be a benefit to all society. There was also a paragraph on making changes to existing laws. Lincoln stated that he would defer to the wisdom of the founders of these laws, unless someone other than him challenged them. If challenged, he would then be willing to consider which would be the greater benefit of justice for all, to change an existing law or to maintain the current one. In effect, Lincoln presented himself as a man who knew his limitations and who had the wisdom to go with his strengths. Moreover, he was one who knew and understood the value of expedient commercial improvements for the citizens. Thus, he was, at twenty-three years old, a man of sagacity.

"I AM A HUMBLE MAN": THE BIRTH OF A POLITICIAN

Nevertheless, the most interesting part of the document about his candidacy is in Lincoln's final paragraphs that directly cite his humbleness and his youthfulness to serve the citizens of Sangamon County. *This first use of his public persona* became a hallmark of most of his campaigns for office. While they can be evaluated as persuasive devices to win the sympathy of the voter, they stand alone as statements that are true to Lincoln as a person and as one who *had* lived a humble life. They are not invented, although the inventiveness is in the selection of these traits to present to the public.

In effect, Lincoln made a personal statement about "his peculiar ambition" to run for public office. "*I was born and have ever remained in the most humble walks of life*" and "*have no wealthy or popular relations to recommend me.*" He is also a person who can accept defeat: "*I have been too familiar with disappointment to be very much chagrined*" if voters did not elect him.[210] It is a statement that could win a voter's sympathy and empathy, especially for those who knew the harshness of life from living in newer and rural areas of the county. The frontier was never far from the experience of eking out a civilized existence in the early half of the nineteenth century in the Midwest.

In most if not all his subsequent campaigns in Illinois, Lincoln represented himself thusly, as a humble man of shortcomings and as

85

one who has known the lowest economic state of life. At this early stage of his political career, it was his only genuine option. He was a not-well-educated young man; he had a frontier upbringing and was in the process of inventing himself. Later, even after he had gained some renown locally as a lawyer and legislator, he cultivated this persona. His circuit riding, almost six months out of each year, gained him popularity in local towns; he had a kind of "plain folks" and an "unabashed" persona that appealed to many. It was a common-man image of one who had "pulled himself up by his bootstraps." And indeed this was the case in the famous debates with Douglas in 1858. Two scholars in particular, Richard Hofstadter and Waldo Braden traced this consistent pattern in Lincoln's presentation-of-self to the public. Hofstadter concluded that the "first author of the Lincoln legend" of the humble, self-made, common man "was Lincoln himself." [211]

Lincoln's Appearance as a First Impression

Once Abe Lincoln committed to campaigning for public office, he not only was speaking to audiences, but also "appearing" before him. This nonverbal message is the first impression an audience receives. Physically, Lincoln at twenty-three was an unusual figure. Taller than most men, his arms were longer, his hands and feet were bigger. In 1834, when one of his closest friends, Joshua Speed, first met Lincoln, he described him as a "long, gawky, ugly, shapeless man." [212] Robert Wilson described him as somewhat "stoop shouldered, his legs were long, feet large, arms longer than any man I ever knew when standing straight.... his arms were unusually long for his height 6'4"; the points of his fingers would touch a point lower on his legs by nearly three inches than usual with other persons." [213] During this same period Abner Ellis described Lincoln as appearing "odd" before a Sangamon audience, wearing a jeans coat too tight for him and pantaloon pants too short for his legs. [214]

Lincoln generally presented this impression even when he wore a suit. Twenty-six years later, when he appeared at Cooper Union to deliver a formal speech in New York, his new black suit seemed ill -

fitting for his body, and he seemed physically unusual to his audience. Charles C. Nott, one of the planners for the event, said that his first impression of Lincoln caused him to expect, "something weird, rough and uncultivated." His appearance "did not fit in with a New York audience's conception of a finished statesman."[215]

Lincoln's substance made the final Impression

Typically, also, of Lincoln as a speaker was that the initial physical impression often diminished as he began to speak. In 1834, Caleb Carman said that his first impression was that Lincoln was a "greenhorn," but after he began to speak, "I found him to be a very intelligent young man.".[216]

The same was true of the New York audience at Cooper Union which hailed his speech, in 1860, as one of the most important of its times, according Lincoln a standing ovation. Some audience members rushed to the stage to shake his hand.[217] Four New York newspapers published the complete text of his speech the following day.[218] The Republicans, who originally had invited Lincoln to speak, developed a tour for him through Connecticut, New Hampshire and Massachusetts.[219] Initially, he was perceived as a "Prairie Orator" because of his fame in the debates with Douglas and because of his "House Divided" speech. When he ended the speech, he became known as a statesman, the result of astute analysis, evidence and argument against the extension of slavery. In 1860, that was the experienced lawyer and politician Lincoln had become. His political journey, however, began with the campaign of 1832.

Lincoln Begins His Political Career: 1832

Lincoln's first attempt to run for a seat in the legislature was interrupted by the Black Hawk war, an event that involved him for ninety days in the service of the army. When he returned to New Salem in mid-July of 1832, Lincoln had less than three weeks to campaign for the office of representative. Although he lost the election, he gained strong endorsement from New Salem citizens with 277 out of 300 votes, even though he placed eighth among the candidates. His platform included positions favorable to New Salem's prosperity: internal improvements such as facilitating navigation along the Sangamon river, better educational facilities, and a law to limit interest rates.[220] The campaign gave him much needed public speaking experience and spread his name throughout the county.

In 1834, Lincoln again campaigned for the office of representative to the Illinois legislature, and learned the value of bipartisan support. Abner Ellis heard him speak during the 1834 campaign and stated that Lincoln said, "I presume you all know who I am. I am humble Abraham Lincoln."[221] His friend, Justice Bowling Green, a Democrat, urged his fellow Democrats to support Lincoln, and many did. He also learned about political tactics in this campaign when the Democrats told him that they would be willing to drop two of their own men and support him as a ploy to remove John T. Stuart, a prominent Whig from Springfield and good friend to Abe. The Democrats knew of Stuart's ambition to eventually run for Congress and hoped to remove him from the legislative picture with this early move against him.[222] Lincoln told Stuart of this strategy. Stuart, confident of his leadership as a Whig in Sangamon County, told Lincoln to agree to this ploy. In turn, Stuart directed a strong campaign against Democrat, Richard Quinton, which resulted in a loss for the Democrats and a better win for the Whigs, who gained Lincoln and John Dawson, as well as Stuart in the legislature.[223] In this campaign, probably because of the bipartisan strategy, Lincoln engaged groups and people individually and made fewer speeches.

A frontier campaign occasionally demanded more from a candidate than a speech. In one instance, Lincoln came to Rowan Herndon's farm at harvest time and helped thirty men to harvest wheat. Rowan had introduced him, and the men said they would vote for him if he could prove himself in harvesting. Lincoln surpassed them in cradling (cutting) wheat and thus won their vote.[224] At another gathering, while he was speaking, Lincoln saw his friend Rowan Herndon physically attacked by a man. Lincoln stepped into the crowd, grabbed the man by his neck and seat of his pants and threw him down, thus restoring order. Then he returned to the front of the crowd and continued his speech.[225]

Lincoln's First Term

Lincoln's first term in the Illinois State legislature began in December 1834, in Vandalia. In its sixteenth year as a state, Illinois' population numbered about 200,000 residents. Representatives were used to "logrolling," bartering votes for legislation favorable to their communities. Deliberating on statewide issues was not as prevalent on the frontier legislative agenda. Increasingly, however, with the growth in population, state issues began to dominate the legislative agenda.

Agriculture, the chief economy, depended on transportation to other markets for economic progress to take place. This meant a system of roads, bridges, canals and railroads was needed to reach eastern and southern outlets of commerce. The 1834-1835 sessions were dominated by the state's need to develop legislation and implement a system of canals from the interior of Illinois to Michigan via the Great Lakes and the Erie Canal to the Atlantic coast.[226]

In his first session, John Stuart mentored Lincoln. Stuart, the leader of the Whig minority, asked him to share his lodgings. Consequently, Lincoln met and engaged in discussion with a number of legislators seeking Stuart's help. The two friends worked in tandem, with Lincoln covering the assembly proceedings in order to free Stuart for leadership duties on committees. On his fifth day in the assembly, Lincoln announced that he would file a bill to limit the jurisdiction of Justices of the Peace. Later, he introduced bills to build a bridge near New Salem and to locate a road northeast of New Salem. Lincoln also learned about parliamentary procedure and house rules, and he became widely acquainted with legislative writing as he handwrote several bills for the congress. By the final weeks of the legislative session, Lincoln was named to twelve special committees, an unusual amount for a first term representative and strong testimony of his effectiveness with fellow legislators.[227]

In the legislature, while in the process of making laws, Lincoln interacted with a wide variety of men, some quite different from the types he knew from his frontier and rural experience. Some representatives were highly educated and wealthy; others had less formal education than Lincoln. Some were heavy drinkers and gamblers, others were rough mannered or refined men, and there were a few teetotalers.[228]

Lincoln's Second Term

In his campaign for a second term, Lincoln included suffrage for women. In the *Sangamo Journal* of June 18, 1836, Lincoln stated, "I go for admitting *all whites* to the right of suffrage, who pay taxes or bear arms (by no means excluding females.)" [229] In 1836, along with sixty-six new members, Lincoln was re-elected to another term in office. Because there were so many new legislators being seated, Lincoln discovered that despite serving only one term, he had become a part of the senior legislative majority. This shift to seniority status redefined his stature with the State Legislature.[230]

Lincoln's second term in the General Assembly included a drawn-out conflict between the Democrats and the Whigs over the issue of the nominating convention. The Democrats, the majority party, held a convention to secure the nomination of Martin Van Buren for President. This was a political maneuver to avoid the fragmentation of loyalties to other candidates and to maintain the cohesiveness of its members for a generally accepted candidate. The political convention, practiced by some parties in the East, often led to a majority of electoral votes. The Whigs favored a freer method that caused them to favor more than one candidate. They supported Daniel Webster in New England, William Henry Harrison in Pennsylvania, and Hugh White in Tennessee. In this way they could block the development of a majority in the Electoral College.[231]

The Democrats introduced legislation to make the convention system mandatory for all parties in Illinois, and the Whigs engaged in counter strategies to kill a vote on the measure. The Democrats won. Lincoln was much involved in these skirmishes and often served as floor manager, replacing John Stuart. Internal improvements were still a dominant issue in these sessions, especially with an emphasis on roads, railroads and canals in that order of importance.[232]

Lincoln's Third Term: The Emergence of the "Long Nine"

This became the longest session the General Assembly had in its early history, three months. Lincoln emerged as a clear leader of the Whigs in the House. Population shifts, reapportionment, and the urgency of internal improvements continued as the major issues, but the "Long Nine" made the removal of the capital from Vandalia to Springfield a key issue as well.

Sangamon County received the highest number of representation in the assembly because it represented the greatest amount of population, with seven representatives in the House and three in the Senate. The power had shifted to the Whigs in Sangamon County. Lincoln emerged as the highest vote getter in his County. He and six other representatives and two Senators formed an alliance designed to make Springfield the permanent capital of Illinois. All nine men were six feet or above, hence, the "Long Nine" appellation; Lincoln the youngest member, at six feet, four inches was among the tallest.[233]

During this session, Stephen Douglas and other Democrats in an effort to resolve the state's transportation needs, developed an all-inclusive internal improvement bill for the development of roads, railroads, canals, navigation expansion of rivers, etc., throughout the state. The Whigs found this an ideal bill for bargaining with members of every county. All parties favored internal improvements, and the "Long Nines" formed strategies to bargain transportation support in exchange for favorable votes for Springfield as state capital. Inevitably the bill grew so large that it had to be rewritten for coherency before a vote could be taken.

Lincoln, as the Whig floor leader, led the Whigs in deal making. He had friendly visits with members in the assembly hall; he met them at taverns; and he held strategy sessions with the "Long Nine" members in order to develop mutual strong support for both bills.

John Taylor, however, a strong advocate for the town of Petersburg, a rival to New Salem, introduced a bill splitting off the northern part of Sangamon County in order to make it a separate county. This jeopardized the Whig votes for Springfield. Lincoln and others developed a compromise strategy. Part of northern Sangamon and part of the adjoining Morgan County could combine as another county. Lincoln forged this through committee meetings and private sessions. The measure passed the House and was killed in the Senate through the efforts of Archer G. Herndon, one of the "Long Nine" members. [234]

The next wave of opposition came from Usher F. Linden, a supporter of keeping the capital in Vandalia. He introduced a bill for a comprehensive investigation of the State Bank that was located in Springfield. Because the Democrats were in the majority on committees, they potentially could ruin any of the designs of the "Long Nine." Moreover, the Democrats did not favor a State Bank. Lincoln recognized that such legislation could place the State Bank in jeopardy. He and Linder maintained a running dispute for several days, while bank officials supplied Lincoln with facts and figures. Finally, both sides agreed that a limited investigation would be conducted. From this, the State Bank earned a clean bill of health. [235]

With this settled it seemed that a vote on the Internal Improvements bill and the State Capital measure would be imminent. Instead, the vote was delayed because Governor Joseph Duncan asked the General Assembly to address the complaints of the Southern states about the distribution of abolitionist literature. They asked the northern states to prohibit the mailing and distribution of abolitionist literature in their states. At Duncan's request, the legislature developed a joint committee of the House and Senate that condemned the abolitionists, that declared the Constitution of United States allowed Southern states to have slaves as property, and also, that stated that the Federal government had no right to abolish slavery in Washington D.C. unless its citizens requested it.

Lincoln was influential in getting the committee to stipulate the statement about citizens requesting its abolishment in Washington

D.C. Otherwise, he refrained from propounding his position against slavery as did others, so as not to jeopardize their bargaining for votes on the new capital and also, because a number of representatives had lived in the south before they came to Illinois. He and five others, however, voted as a minority against this resolution.[236]

After this, the Internal Improvements bill passed the House and Senate. It passed at a staggering budget of seven and a half million dollars, millions more than the state budget. Ultimately, the bill put the state of Illinois in debt for forty-five years. The only project to be fully completed was the Illinois to Michigan canal. Many other proposed roads, canals and bridges were not completed. The state of Illinois was finally able to clear this debt in 1882.[237]

When the state capital bill came before the House, a parliamentary battle developed that delayed the vote. Lincoln worked to counter every move of the opposition. Robert Wilson, Lincoln's fellow representative from Sangamon County worked with him on this issue. Wilson noted, "The contest on this bill was long and hard." [238] In the meantime, Lincoln suggested to Alex Dunbar of Coles County that he introduce an amendment to the bill requiring that the chosen city provide two acres for government buildings and $50,000 to develop the move. Wealthy patrons in Springfield readily agreed to put forth the money. Lincoln knew that the other competitors for the capital, Vandalia, Alton, Peoria, Illiopolis, and Jacksonville, could not muster this kind of financial largesse. The amendment was adopted by a vote of 56 to 25.[239]

Twice, the opposition offered a motion to table the entire bill, and the second one won a vote on this measure to defer it to July 4, 1837, when the legislature would not be in session. It passed by a margin of one vote. Proponents of Springfield despaired for it appeared that the opposition had won at this point. There was an operational rule, however, in the legislature that when something is "indefinitely postponed, [it] requires a vote of reconsideration."

Lincoln refused to concede. He conferred with his colleagues, said he refused to give up hope, and argued that a margin of one vote was not decisive. He directed the "Long Nine" men to approach specific people and also, to find those who were absent for this vote and to return to the assembly.[240] The measure was overturned and then the balloting began. On the fourth ballot, Springfield cleared with a majority vote of 73 to 50 and the wealthier citizens of Springfield began to pledge the $50,000.[241]

A few days before the close of the assembly (March 4, 1837) Lincoln and one other "Long Niner," Dan Stone, expressed themselves on the slavery resolutions that they had passed six weeks earlier. They circulated their position to the representatives that was read and published in the *House Journal of Illinois.* They went on record to state that the institution of slavery was both an injustice and bad policy, that the "promulgation of the abolition doctrine tends to increase than to abate its evils." They agreed that although Congress had no power under the Constitution to interfere with slavery in the different states, it could abolish it in the District off Columbia if its citizens so wished.

Dan Stone and Abraham Lincoln, both from Sangamon County, signed the statement that appears in the *House Journal of Illinois Legislature,* 1836-1837, pp. 817, 818.[242]

Abraham Lincoln, at the age of 28, emerged as a highly seasoned politician. He had achieved another layer of learning.

CHAPTER TWENTY

Lincoln's Emergence as a Storyteller

So much about Lincoln, during his first twenty-seven years of life, was unique and highly individual. Outstanding among his greatest strengths was his storytelling skills. Throughout his life, Lincoln developed and honed his ability to weave wisdom, witticism and relevance into his tales. He began to develop this skill by watching and listening to his father hold the attention of others when telling the stories he was noted for. Later, Lincoln would go out and practice his newly learned storytelling lessons on his peers.

One of his favorite Pigeon Creek stories that seemed to win him acceptance with adults as well as with his peers, was his oft-repeated "Lizard Story" about a Baptist minister. The minister dressed in coarse linen which had a few buttons to hold his pants together and one or two for his shirt. While preaching the text "I am the Christ whom I shall represent today," he felt a lizard crawling up his leg. First he slapped at his legs, but the creature eluded him, so he unbuttoned his pants. By this time it was crawling up his back so he unbuttoned his shirt collar, continuing to preach while literally baring himself to the congregation. While a dazed congregation looked on, an old lady took one look at him and said, "Well, if you represent Christ I am done believing in the Bible." He sometimes used this anecdote in his early stump speeches.[243]

Shortly after he arrived, New Salem residents came to know Lincoln when he worked as a clerk for an election. When the day slowed down, Lincoln began to tell jokes and stories.[244] Lincoln gained acceptance with his humor and jokes. People in New Salem knew him first as a humorist and later as a serious thinker and speaker. When he first debated they expected him to tell stories. Instead he put forth serious arguments about the topic.

Joseph Gillespie, a fellow lawyer and political friend, noted that Lincoln used anecdotes as "labor saving contrivances. He could convey his ideas on any subject through the form, of a simple story or homely illustration with better effect than any man I ever knew. To illustrate: I was talking to him once about state sovereignty. He said that the advocates of that theory always reminded him of the fellow who contended that the proper place for the big kettle was inside of the little one."[245]

He understood the value of entertainment and levity when communicating a thought or concept. By the careful selection of words, he was able to dramatize and communicate information that might not have resonated as well with a mere statement of facts. "My policies are short and sweet like an old woman's dance," said Lincoln when he announced his candidacy for state representative.[246]

Lincoln's storytelling established a reputation in Sangamon County. When his legislative sessions ended for the year he would return to surveying. Often while laying out new roads or new towns, a number of men and boys volunteered to help him carry chains, drive stakes and blaze trees in order to hear him tell his stories. Occasionally, they would organize a picnic.[247]

Abner Ellis said that Lincoln's stories "made his company desirable by a great many young members of the legislature as well as the rising young lawyers." [248] In a discussion about patronage and the demand for positions from politicians, Lincoln acknowledged that there were too many people who felt they were qualified for promotions and high positions. "That reminds me of a story I heard in a small town in Illinois…. Every man in town owned a fast horse, each one considered his own the fastest, so to decide the matter there was to be a trial of all the horses to take place at the same time. An old man living in the town known as 'Uncle' was selected as umpire. When it was over each one anxious for his decision, the old man putting his hands behind his back, said, 'I have come to one conclusion, that when there are so many fast horses in one little town none are any great shakes.' " [249]

As a circuit riding lawyer, Lincoln and some of his fellow lawyers spent evenings exchanging stories and jokes. As Henry C. Whitney pointed out, some men spent their leisure time drinking or gambling. Lincoln, Judge David Davis and some of the other lawyers would spend their evenings trading stories among themselves and with local citizens of the towns they serviced. One such discussion involved the concept of metempsychosis, a doctrine that when one person dies, a child inherits the soul of the departing one. One of the lawyers whom they called Quirk, not of their circuit, was well known for his meanness. Several people participating in the discussion of metempsychosis had negative things to say about Quirk. Gradually, they realized that Lincoln had been silent, and Judge Davis said, "Queer doctrine! Queer doctrine!! Eh! Lincoln?" Whereupon Lincoln replied, "I rather reckon, that's good doctrine, and it's nothin' agin' it, that when Quirk was born, no one died."[250]

Lincoln's early exposure to writings in the Bible and other books such as Aesop's *Fables* helped him to understand the use of parable and double meanings to effectively deliver a message. Years later after Lincoln delivered his "House Divided" speech and won national attention, he was able to use the famous line with telling effect in the debates with Stephen Douglas. "I say that 'A house divided against itself cannot stand.' Does the Judge [Douglas] say it *can* stand? [Laughter]....I would like to know if it is his opinion that a house divided against itself *can stand*.... If he does, then there is a question of veracity, not between him and me, but between the Judge and an authority of a somewhat higher character." [Laughter and applause][251]

Of greater importance to Lincoln was the effect of using humor to help himself. Not only did his humor commend him to others, teach a point, or lend effectiveness to an argument, but it also served as a form of tension release for himself. His good friend Joshua Speed observed that Lincoln's "reputation for telling anecdotes...was in my judgment necessary to his very existence....Hence he sought relaxation in anecdotes." [252] Lincoln confirmed this to his law partner

William Herndon while discussing his tendency toward depression: "If it were not for these stories—jokes—jests—I should die; they give vent—are the vents—of my moods and gloom." [253]

Becoming a Lawyer and Moving to Springfield

Lincoln Moves to Springfield and Becomes a Lawyer

Lincoln's world had expanded beyond New Salem. With his election in 1834, John L. Stuart had suggested that Lincoln begin to read Illinois law in order to become licensed. Lincoln began in earnest to study Stuart's law books, and continued to read law until he received his license in September, 1836, from the state of Illinois. After that, in 1837, Lincoln moved to Springfield, the new capital of Illinois, to become a partner in Stuart's law firm. When Stuart ran for a congressional seat and won, Lincoln operated the law office until Stuart returned to private life.

Post New Salem

Lincoln spent the next twenty-four years of his life, before his presidency, engaged in the legal and political world, continually engrossed in analysis of legal cases and issues to seek the best arguments and evidence for his clients and political constituency. He spent much of his time analyzing cases, writing briefs, and presenting his cases before juries. During this same period, he diligently spent several hours a week in the state library researching statutes and working for the Whig party to draft legislation, or to prepare to debate issues in the assembly. He sought consensus from committee discussions, debated in the chambers of the state legislature and frequently spoke to the public. On a day-to-day basis for the remainder of his life he was never far from the search for the key argument to present the best case he could. From his first debate in New Salem, Lincoln was known as one who began with the analysis of a case or issue before he discovered the arguments he would use. Judge David Davis the chief judge of the Eighth District circuit court which included Lincoln, noted that Abe "studied where the truth of a thing lay and so acted on his conviction: bent his whole soul to that idea and end." [254]

Finding the "truth of a thing"

Lincoln's most notable argument, traceable to his early childhood, developed when he reentered politics as a Republican after the repeal of the compromise of 1850. He could no longer say that gradual emancipation was the answer to slavery and the intention of the founding fathers. The admission of new states threatened its expansion, not its extinction. Thus he argued that "A house divided against itself cannot stand," which, of course, came from the Bible.

During his senatorial debates with Stephen Douglas, Lincoln had diligently prepared notebooks of arguments and evidence. Yet he was unable to do much more than counter-assert Douglas' contention that the Founding Fathers implicitly meant that slavery could be extended to the new territories.[255]

When Lincoln received the invitation in October 1859, to speak in New York on February 27, 1860, at Cooper Union, he began a more extensive, comprehensive search to answer Douglas' charge that the Founding Fathers supported the extension of slavery.

He studied the original proceedings and debates of the first congressional meetings that led to the development and approval of the Constitution. These were Jonathan Elliot's *Debates in the Several State Conventions on the Adoption of the Federal Constitution, The Congressional Globe,* and the *Annuals of Congress.* He began to marshal proof against Douglas by examining the votes of the signers of the Constitution each time the topic of extension of slavery emerged. The new nation of thirteen states also had jurisdiction over the Northwest Territory. In 1784, four of the signers excluded slavery from the Northwest Territory. Then he examined the participation of other signers in 1787-1788 and during the first session of the Continental Congress after the Constitution was signed and after twelve amendments were added. He found a clear majority of twenty-one of the thirty-nine signers who had voted to exclude the territories as part of their federal responsibility. Other than one or two pro-slavery southerners, the others did not vote for extension of slavery to the territories.[256]

At Cooper Union, Lincoln made Douglas' contention the text of his speech: "Our fathers, when they framed the Government under which we live, understood the question [of extending slavery] just as well, and even better than we do now." Lincoln posed this question: "Does the federal government have the right to control the extension of slavery to the territories?" He answered the question by the proof he found in the meetings and debates of the Founding Fathers. Ultimately, Lincoln's research and razor-sharp arguments and analysis in this speech won him national attention and led to his nomination for the Presidency.

Lincoln's Educational Experience

Lincoln's education of formal learning, informal self-directed learning, and his life experiences from 1809 to 1837, assumed a layering process, a dynamic which allowed for periods of time between major study bouts for Lincoln to absorb and test his learning. For someone like him who needed to reflect and digest new learning, it seemed to be a "goodness of fit," commensurate with his physical and mental development from child to adult. His New Salem years taught him that he could make the transition from physical labor to a life based on his mental abilities. Because of his intellect and capacity to abstract beyond the frontier rudiments of his life, Lincoln's twenty-eight years of frontier education, his self-discipline and his self-directed study prepared him sufficiently to enter and compete in the larger world of politics and law, and ultimately, the Presidency.

Lincoln's American Life Experience

Few men of Lincoln's time would have had the will and mentality to overcome the lack of opportunities that Lincoln faced. Nor would they have chosen to live so poorly while studying and preparing for a career. His frontier upbringing served him well. During his early struggles to fulfill his emotional and material needs, Lincoln discovered the life of the mind. If he was slower to develop than some, he was the better for it as it gave him time to absorb and ascertain that he had mastered the learning.

In tandem with Lincoln's development and self-learning, his frontier experience helped him to understand how a democratic society can evolve. In the Pigeon Creek area, he witnessed the establishment of a modicum of cooperation with his neighbors. These first steps of accommodation gradually led his neighbors to become a more cohesive community that tried to adhere to the democratic principles of individual freedom and the basic establishment of a free society.

Pigeon Creek, Indiana, and New Salem, Illinois, both fledgling communities, gave Lincoln authentic experience and understanding about the struggle and progression a democratic society undergoes to champion a Bill of Rights and to abide by constitutional principles. Ultimately, Abraham Lincoln, a son of the frontier, became the leader who tested the integrity of the Bill of Rights and the Constitution.

Rendering of Abraham Lincoln as a young lawyer

ENDNOTES

CHAPTER ONE: Frontier Life Dispositions

[1] Arnold Gesell, M.D. "Introduction," Louis A. Warren, *Lincoln's Youth,* Indiana 1816 Years, -1830 (Indianapolis: Indiana Historical Society Press, 1959), p. xxi.

CHAPTER TWO: A Fundamental Change in Environment

[2] John Y. Simon, "House Divided: Lincoln and His father," Tenth Annual R. Gerald McMurtry Lecture, Ft. Wayne, Ind.: Louis A. Warren Lincoln Library and Museum, 1987, p.5.

[3] Kenneth J. Winkle, *The Young Eagle,* The Rise of Abraham Lincoln (Dallas: Taylor Trade Publishing, 2001), p.13.

[4] David Herbert Donald, *Lincoln* (New York: Simon and Schuster: 1995) pp.24-25.

[5] Nathaniel Grigsby Interview by William H. Herndon, Sept. 13, 1865, *Herndon's Informants,* Edited by Douglas L. Wilson and Rodney O. Davis (Urbana: University of Illinois Press, 1998), p.111.

[6] Charles H. Coleman, "The Half-faced Camp in Indiana Fact or Myth?" *Abraham Lincoln Quarterly,* 7 (September, 1952), 138-146.

[7] Coleman, p.140.

[8] *Collected Works of Abraham Lincoln,* 1, Roy P. Basler, Editor (New Brunswick: Rutgers University Press, 1955), p.386.

CHAPTER THREE: The Death of Nancy Hanks Lincoln

[9] Warren, pp. 52-53.

[10] J.T. Hobson, *Footprints of Abraham Lincoln* (Dayton: The Otterbein Press, 1909), p.19.

[11] Dennis Hanks Interview with Wm. Herndon, *HI*, p.40.

[12] Philip D. Jordan, "The Death of Nancy Hanks Lincoln," *Indiana Magazine of History* 40, (June, 1944), 103-110.

[13] Doris Kearns Goodwin, *Team of Rivals* (New York: Simon and Schuster, 2005), p. 48.

[14] Bernard Brommel, Ph.D. Interview with the author. February 20, 2009.

[15] Dennis Hanks, Interview with WHH, *HI.* p. 40.

[16] Michael Burlingame, *The Inner World of Abraham Lincoln* (Urbana: University of Illinois Press, 1997), p. 94. Burlingame cites Clarence W. Bell in an address delivered in Lerna, Ill., *Weekly Eagle,* 7 November, 1930. Bell claimed that he was closely related to Sarah Bush Lincoln.

[17] Henry R. Rankin, *Personal Recollections of Abraham Lincoln* (New York: G. Putnam's Sons, 1916), pp. 320-323.

[18] Burlingame, p. 95.

CHAPTER FOUR: The Stabilizing Influence of Sarah Bush Lincoln

[19] Dennis F. Hanks, Int. with WHH, *HI.* , Jan. 13, 1865, p. 99; See also, Sarah Bush Lincoln Interview with WHH, *HI.* , Sept. 8, 1865, p. 106.

[20] Warren, p. 64.

[21] Sarah Bush Johnson, Interview with WHH, *HI.* , p .106.

[22] Augustus H. Chapman Written Statement, *HI.* , Sept. 8, 1865, p. 97.

[23] Warren, pp. 71-75.

[24] Donald, p. 27.

[25] Sarah B. Lincoln, *HI.* , p.107.

[26] Donald, pp. 30-31.

[27] A. Chapman, *HI.* , p. 36.

CHAPTER FIVE: Verbalness and the Lincoln Family

[28] William H. Herndon and Jesse Weik, *Herndon's Life of Lincoln* (Cleveland: The World Publishing Co., 1943), p. 3.

[29] Dennis Hanks, *HI.* , 37; Chapman, *HI.* , p.96.

[30] John Hanks, Interview with William H. Hendon, 1865-1866, *HI,* p. 54.

[31] Dennis Hanks, *HI,.* p. 37.

[32] William G. Greene, Letter to William H. Herndon, Dec. 20, 1865, *HI., p.145.*

[33] Donald, p. 23: Warren, p. 8 and p. 53: Warren inspected the Sparrow will, Spenser Courthouse *Wills,* 1818.

[34] Dennis Hanks, Int. with WHH Sept. 8, 1865, *HI.* , p. 105.

[35] Nathaniel Grigsby, Interview with William H. Herndon, *HI.* , Sept. 12, 1865, p. 114.

[36] *Abraham Lincoln His Story in His Own Words,* edited with notes by Ralph Geoffrey Newman (Garden City: Doubleday and Co., 1945), p. 11.

[37] Dennis Hanks, *HI.,* p.37; Warren, pp. 10-11. Lincoln cited his mother's teachings: See Rankin, *Recollections...p. 320.*

[38] Warren, p. 10.

[39] Sarah B. Lincoln, *HI.,* p. 107.

[40] Dennis Hanks, *HI.,* p. 38.
[41] D. Hanks, *HI.,* p. 37.
[42] D. Hanks, *HI.,* p. 37.
[43] Gesell, xvii.

CHAPTER SIX: Reading, Writing and Ciphering in Kentucky

[44] *Abraham Lincoln,* p. 9.
[45] Samuel Haycraft, Letter to William H. Herndon, June 1865, *HI.* , p. s67.
[46] Warren, pp. 28-30; Warren inspected the textbooks Abe used and it is his
    discussion and analysis of this reading material for study that the author
    refers to. The author's familiarity is with the elocution books Warren
    discusses.
[47] Warren, p. 29.
[48] Warren, p. 28-29.
[49] Warren, p. 81.
[50] D. Hanks, *HI.,* p. 38.
[51] Warren, p. 11.
[52] Haycraft, p. 503; Erastus Burba, Letter to William H. Herndon, *HI.,* April 2,
    l866, p. 241.
[53] Warren, p. 11.

CHAPTER SEVEN: Reading and Studying: Maintaining the Process of Self-Learning

[54] Hobson, *Footprints...,* p. 19.
[55] Warren, pp. 35-36.
[56] Warren, pp. 86-87.
[57] Warren, p. 25.
[58] Mentor Graham, Interview with William H. Herndon, *HI.,* 1865-1866, p. 450.
[59] Lincoln is quoted in Oliver C. Terry, Letter to Jesse W. Weik, July, 1888, *HI.,*
    p. 662.
[60] David Turnham, Interview with William H. Herndon, Sept. 15, 1865, *HI.,* p.
    121.
[61] Warren, pp. 76-80.
[62] Sarah B. Lincoln, *HI.,* p. 108.
[63] Warren, pp. 125-127.
[64] Chauncy Hobart, *Recollections of My Life,* Fifty Years of Itinerancy in the
    Northwest (Red Wing Printing Co., l885), p. 71; also cited in Warren, p.
    243.

[65]Allen Thorndike Rice, *Reminiscences of Abraham Lincoln by Distinguished Men of His Times.* (New York: 1888), p. 458.

[66] Isaac N. Arnold, *The Life of Abraham Lincoln,* 3rd sed. (Chicago: Jansen, McCurdy and Co., 1885), p. 25.

[67] Warren, p. 136 and p. 247.

CHAPTER EIGHT: Becoming a Self-Learner and Becoming a Hired Hand

[68] Sarah B. Lincoln, *HI.,* p. 106.

[69] David Turnham, Letter to WHH, Sept. 16, 1865, p. 129.

[70] Warren, pp. 197-201.

[71] Sarah B. Lincoln, *HI.,* p. 107.

[72] Warren, p. 168.

[77] Wood, p. 124.

[78] Elizabeth Crawford, Interview with William H. Herndon, Sept. 16, 1865, *HI.,* p. 126.

[79] Donald, pp. 34-35.

[80] Green B. Taylor, Interview with William H. Herndon, Sept. 16, 1865, *HI.,* pp. 129-130.

[81] Anne Roby Gentry, Interview with William H. Herndon, Sept. 17, 1865, pp. 131-32; see also, Burlingame, pp.123-124.

CHAPTER NINE: Two Major Events at Nineteen: Death of Sarah Lincoln Grigsby and a Trip to New Orleans

[82] Burlingame, pp. 95-96; Warren, p. 174.

[83] Newspaper article from *Indianapolis News,* April 12, 1902, reprinted in Hobson, *Footprints...,* p .24.

[84] Warren, pp. 175-186.

[85] Anne R. Gentry, Interview with WHH, *HI.,* p. 131; Warren, p. 184.

[86] Absalom Gentry, son of Allen and Anne Gentry, reported Lincoln's remark, saying that he heard it from his father. See Warren, p. 261. If Lincoln didn't say this on his first visit to New Orleans, he may have said it on his second trip.

CHAPTER TEN: Facing Another Frontier

[87] Warren, pp. 175-186.

[88] Wood, p. 124.

[89] Dennis Hanks, Interview with Erastus Wright, Chicago, June 1865, *HI.*, p. 27.

[90] Warren, p. 204.

[91] John Hanks, statements collected by Herndon, in Hertz, *Hidden Lincoln*, p. 347.

[92] A.H. Chapman, written statement to Herndon, Sept. 8, 1865, *HI.*, p. 102; see also, Lincoln's "Autobiography," excerpted in *The Lincoln Reader*, ed. by Paul M. Angle, pp. 36-37.

[93] J. Hanks, in Hertz, p. 347.

[94] J. Hanks, Interview with WHH, Chicago, June 13, 1865, in *HI.*, pp. 43-44.

CHAPTER ELEVEN: Abe at Twenty-One: Self-Learning and Life Experiences: Physical, Intellectual and Emotional Development

[95] John Romine, quoted in Herndon and Weik, p. 38.

[96] Dennis Hanks, Interview by Francis F. Browne, *Everyday Life of Abraham Lincoln*, p. 33.

[98] A. Lincoln to Joshua F. Speed: Speed Interview with WHH, 1866, *HI.*, p. 499.

[99] Matilda Johnston Moore, Interview with WHH, Sept. 8, 1865, *HI.*, p. 109.

[100] N. Grigsby, Int. with WHH, Sept. 12, 1865, *HI.*, p. 113.

[101] Warren, p. 245: Warren reproduced this statement for John P. Gulliver, *The Independent* (New York) Sept. 11, 1864. Gulliver had heard Lincoln speak at Norwich, Connecticut on March 9th. He met Lincoln the next day and interviewed him, asking him "How did you get this unusual power of putting things?" Gulliver thought it was the way Lincoln was educated, but Lincoln gave the above answer revealing his mental processes.

[102] A. Gesell, in Warren, xix.

[103] Gesell, xx.

[104] Hanks quoted in Browne, pp. 54-55.

[105] Samuel A. Crawford, Letter to WHH, January 4, 1866, in Hertz, *Hidden Lincoln*, p. 285; see also, Elizabeth Crawford and her anecdote about Lincoln bothering his sister and her friends and she admonished him, saying that he should be ashamed of himself and what did he expect to become: "Be President of the United States," he said. E. Cawford, Interview with WHH, *HI.*, pp. 126-127.

[106] Sarah B. Lincoln, Int. with WHH, *HI.*, p. 107; Green B. Taylor, Interview with WHH, September 16, 1865, in *HI.*, p. 130.; John Hanks, Interview with WHH, 1865-1866, in *HI.*, p. 455.

[107] N. Grigsby, *HI.*, p. 113.

[108] K. Duncan and D. F. Nickols, *Mentor Graham*, The Man Who Taught Lincoln. "Graham's Answers to Herndon's Questionnaire," (Chicago: University of Chicago Press, 1944), p. 253; see also, p. 213.

[109] Michael Burlingame, pp. 94-96, and his chapter on "Lincoln's Depressions" pp. 92-122, *Inner World of AL.*; see also Charles B. Stozier, *Lincoln's Quest for Union:* Public and Private Meanings (NY: Basic Books, 1982), pp. 28-30.

[110] D. Donald, *Lincoln,* p. 116.

[111] Abraham Lincoln, Letter to Andrew Johnston, April 18, 1846, *CW* 1: 377-378.

[112] A. Lincoln Letter to Andrew Johnston, September 6, 1846, *CW 1*: 384-389.

[113] Warren, p. 134.

[114] A. Lincoln, Letter to Andrew Johnston, Feb. 24, 1846, *CW* 1: 366-370. This letter includes 24 stanzas of "My Childhood Home I See Again."

[115] N. Grigsby, *HI.,* p. 113.

[116] E. Crawford, *HI.,* p. 126.

[117] W. Wood, *HI.,* p. 124.

[118] Burlingame, pp. 35-36; See footnote on John E. Roll, an Illinois friend of Lincoln, whose reminiscences appeared in Chicago and other Illinois newspapers, p. 117.

[119] A. Lincoln to John D. Johnston, *Item 166 Copy of Agreement,* Oct. 25,1841, *HI.,* p. 227.

[120] A. Lincoln, *Autobiography,* written for John L. Scripps, *CW* IV: 46.

[121] A. Lincoln, Letter to John Johnston, Jan. 12, 1851, CW II: 96-97. He refers to Harriet Chapman's letter, p. 96.

[122] Lincoln to Johnson, *Ibid.,* p. 97.

[123] A. Chapman, *HI.,* p. 137.

CHAPTER TWELVE: From the Mind to the Expression to Others: Developing His Oral Persona

[124] Warren, pp. 98-99.

[125] N. Grigsby, *HI.,* p. 114.

[126] Grigsby, *HI.,* pp. 114-115.

[127] Herndon and Weik, p. 50.

[128] Warren, pp. 193-195.

[129] M. Moore, *HI.,* pp. 109-110.

[130] M. Moore, *HI.,* pp. 109-110.

[131] Elizabeth Crawford, Interview with WHH, Sept. 16, 1865, *HI.,* p. 126.

[132] Warren, p. 211.

[133] Warren, pp. 55-56.

[134] S. T. Johnson Interview with WHH, Sept.14, 1865, *HI.,* p. 115.

CHAPTER THIRTEEN: From the Mind to the Expression to Others: Developing His Written Persona

[135] John Locke Scripps, *Life of Abraham Lincoln,* reprinted, 1900 edition, Cranbrook Press, p.16 (Digitized by Google)

[136] Warren, pp. 55-56; Warren interviewed members of the Elkin family and several members claimed that Lincoln had written a letter requesting him to conduct a service for his mother; one claimed to have seen this letter. See, Warren, p. 229.

[137] Mentor Graham, Interview with WHH, 1865-1866, *HI.,* p. 450.

[138] N. Grigsby, Int. with WHH, Sept. 12, 1865, *HI.,* p. 112.

[139] Warren, pp. 168-169.

[140] William Wood, Interview with WHH, Sept. 15, 1865, *HI.,* pp. 123-124.

[141] Warren, p. 124; p. 169.

[142] See Douglas Wilson and Rodney Davis' note #2, p.135, *HI.* The verse begins with "Time what an empty vapor 'tis."; see also, *Abraham Lincoln: Presidents as Poets,* Virtual Programs and Services, Library of Congress, p. 1.

[143] Joseph Richardson, Int. with WHH, September 14, 1865,*HI.,* pp. 119-120; Herndon learned that the original chapter of "Chronicles of Reuben" was found among the roof timbers in one of the Grigsby family homes by a carpenter; see Herndon, pp. 44-45. James Swaney, carpenter, found a chapter written in Lincoln's handwriting. John W. Lamar to J.W. Wartmann, Jan.3, 1887, *HI.,* pp. 598-599.

[144] S. A. Crawford to WHH, Elizabeth Crawford's memorized version thirty-six years later, in Wertz, *Hidden Lincoln,* pp. 385-287.

[145] See Burlingame, p. 210, footnote 25: Burlingame cites interviews from the Grigsby family as they appear in *The Monitor,* Grandview, Ind. Feb. 13, 1930, and James Gentry's reminiscences, Sept. 1902, Rockport, Indiana; and *Louisville Courier-Journal,* September 28, 1902.

[146] Warren, p. 196; He found Mrs. Betsy Grigsby's interview in the Rockport *Journal,* Feb.12, 1897. See also, Hobson's *Footprints...,* pp. 26-28.

[147] Warren, pp. 196-197.

[148] N. Grigsby, Int. with WHH, *HI.,* p. 114.; See also, Robert Bray, "The Power to Hurt": Lincoln's Early Use of Satire and Invective," *The Journal of the American Lincoln Association.* Un. of Illinois Press, Winter, 1995, vol.16, pp. 39-59.

CHAPTER FOURTEEN: Reading Becomes Lincoln's Window to the World at Twenty-One

[149] Basler, *CW IV*, First debate with Douglas, Aug. 21, 1858, p. 184.

[150] M. Moore, Int. with WHH, *HI.,* p. 109.

[151] William Grimshaw, *A History of the United States from Their First Settlement to the Cession of Florida in Eighteen Hundred and Twenty-One.* (2nd.ed.) Philadelphia: Benjamin Warner Publisher, 1821), pp. 27-33. Google Reprint Online.

[152] Fred Kaplan, *Lincoln: The Biography of a Writer.* (New York: Harper Collins Publisher, 2008), p. 34.

[153] Warren, p. 76.

[154] David Turnham, Int. with WHH. *HI.,* p. 129.

[155] Herndon and Weik, p. 34.

[156] Kaplan, p. 35.

[157] Kaplan, p. 155.

CHAPTER FIFTEEN: Transferring Self-Learning to Illinois: The Final Influence

[158] New Salem, Menard County; Originally it was part of Sangamon County during the years Lincoln resided there.

[159] John Hanks, Interview with WHH, in Hertz, *The Hidden Lincoln,* p. 340.

[160] Clarendon E. Van Norman, *The Rotarian,* Feb. 1963.

[161] J. Hanks, p. 340.

[162] J. Hanks, p. 349.

[163] Mentor Graham, Interview with WHH, May 29, 1865, *HI.,* p. 9.

[164] Graham, p. 9.

[165] Ida M. Tarbell, *The Life of Abraham Lincoln, V*ol. I. (New York: Lincoln Historical Society, Merritt, MCMII, A public domain reprint by BiblioBazaar, LLC.), pp. 62-63.

[166] Graham, p. 10.

[167] William Baringer, *Day By Day*, Vol. I, Editor in Chief, Earl Schenck Miers. (Washington: Lincoln Sesquicentennial Commission, 1960), pp. 15-44.

[168] Tarbell, p. 99.

[169] Baringer, D*ay by Day,* p. 29.

[170] Tarbell, pp. 93-94; Lincoln told this incident to A.J. Conant, an artist who was painting his portrait in 1860, in Springfield, Il. Tarbell cited Conant's article, "My Acquaintance with Abraham Lincoln" in *The Liber Scriptorum.* There is no other documentation that she cites.

[171] Abner Ellis, Statement to WHH, Jan. 23, 1866, *HI.,* p. 173.

[172] K. Duncan and D. R. Nichols, *Mentor Graham*, p. 153.

[173] Duncan and Nichols, pp. 39-56.

[174] Duncan and Nichols, pp. 95-100.

[175] Mentor Graham Interview with WHH, May 29, 1865, *HI.*, p. 10.

[176] Duncan and Nichols, p. 97.

[177] Duncan and Nichols, pp. 129-132.

[178] Duncan and Nichols, p. 129.

[179] Robert B. Rutledge to WHH, Nov. 30, 1866, *HI.*, p. 426.

[180] Henry B. Rankin, *Personal Recollections of Abraham Lincoln.* (New York: G. P. Putnam's Sons, 1916), pp. 11-12.

[181] Graham, *HI.*, p. 10.

[182] Tarbell, p. 100. Carl Sandburg, *Abraham Lincoln: The Prairie and the War Years.* (New York: Harcourt Brace and Co., 1926), pp. 44-46.

[183] Elizabeth Herndon Bell, Interview with WHH, March, 1887, *HI.*, p. 606.

[184] Herndon and Weik, p. 90. Lincoln sent portions of his salary as a Representative in Congress to Herndon to pay off his debts from his New Salem business ventures.

[185] Robert Rutledge, *HI.*, p. 384.

CHAPTER SIXTEEN: Love and Death: Lincoln and Ann Rutledge

[186] Rankin, p. 71.

[187] Jasper Rutledge, Interview with WHH, March 9, 1887, *HI.*, p. 606.

[188] Rankin, p. 72.

[189] R. Rutledge, p. 383.

[190] Rankin, pp. 73-74.

[191] Duncan and Nichols, p. 159.

[192] John Hill to WHH, June 6,1865, *HI.*, p. 25; see also, Harden Bale to WWH, *HI.*, p. 13; Elizabeth Abell to WHH, *HI.*, p. 557.

[193] Rankin, p. 81; see also, Duncan and Nichols, pp. 158-159.

[194] Rankin, pp. 81-83.

[195] William G. Greene, Int. with WHH, May 30, 1865, *HI.*, p. 21

[196] Lincoln said this to Mentor Graham, Duncan and Nickols, p. 175.

CHAPTER SEVENTEEN: Three Mentors: Bowling Green, Jack Kelso and Mentor Graham

[197] Albert A. Woldman, "Attorney and Counselor at Law," *The Lincoln Reader,* ed. by Paul M. Angle (New Brunswick: Rutgers University Press, 1947), pp.

89-92. See also, A. A. Woldman, *Lawyer Lincoln* (Boston: Houghton Mifflin, 1936).

[198] Mary Turner, "Will the Real Jack Kelso Please Stand Up?" *For the People,* A newsletter of the Abraham Lincoln Association, Vol.1, No.4, Winter 1999, Springfield, IL, pp. 1-2.

[199] Tarbell, p. 93.

[200] Hardin Bale, Interview with WHH, 1866, *HI.,* p. 528.

[201] James Short to WHH, July 7, 1865, *HI.,* p. 74.

[202] William G. Greene, Interview with WHH, *HI.,* p. 20.

[203] Stuart, *HI.,* p. 64.

[204] Author's telephone interview with Heidi Brown, Events Coordinator, Lincoln Chamber of Commerce, July 21, 2010.

[205] Duncan and Nickols, p. 201; p. 261.

CHAPTER EIGHTEEEN: Governance and Lincoln: His Learning Experiences from Pigeon Creek and New Salem

(no endnotes)

CHAPTER NINETEEN: Becoming a Politician

[206] Robert B. Rutledge, *HI.,* p. 385.

[207] "Communication to the People of Sangamo County," Roy Basler, *CW* 1, pp. 5-9.

[208] Duncan and Nichols, p. 132.

[209] John McNamar to G. U. Giles, *HI.,* p. 253.

[210] Basler, *CW,* I. p. 8.

[210] Richard Hofstadter, *American Political Traditions* (NY: Alfred A. Knopf, Inc., 1948), p. 94; Waldo W. Braden, *Abraham Lincoln As a Public Speaker* (Baton Rouge: Louisiana State University Press, 1988), pp. 4-9.

[212] Joshua F. Speed, Statement for WHH. *HI.,* p. 588.

[213] Robert L. Wilson Statement to WHH. *HI.,* pp. 201-202.

[214] Abner Y. Ellis, Statement for WHH. *HI.,* January 23, 1866, p. 171.

[215] Charles C. Nott's Statement is reproduced in Ronald C. White Jr., *A. Lincoln* (New York: Random House, 2009) p. 311. Originally Nott's statement was published in *Intimate Memories of Lincoln* (Elmira, NY: Primavera Press, 1945), p. 258.

[216] Caleb Carman, Statement to WHH. *HI,.* November 30, 1866, p. 429.

[217] Benjamin P. Thomas, *Abraham Lincoln.* 3rd ed. (NY: Modern Library, 1968), p. 204.

[218] Braden, p. 56.

[219] Ronald C.White, Jr., *A. Lincoln* pp. 314-315.

[220] Paul Simon, *Lincoln's Preparation for Greatness,* The Illinois Legislative Years (Urbana: Un. of Illinois Press, Illinai Book Edition, 1971, by permission of Un. of Oklahoma Press, 1965), p. 10.

[221] Abner Ellis, Statement for WHH, January 23, 1866, *HI.*, p. 171.

[222] Simon, p. 16.

[223] Simon, p. 17-19.

[224] J. Rowan Herndon, Let. to WHH, *HI.*, May 28, 1865, p. 8.

[225] J. Rowan Herndon, Let. to WHH, *HI.*, June 21, 1865, p. 51.

[226] Wilson, p. 204.

[227] Wilson, p. 204.

[228] Thomas, pp. 62-63.

[229] Lincoln's position on this is reprinted in Simon, p. 43.

[230] Simon, p. 53.

[231] Thomas, pp. 52-53

[232] Thomas, pp. 52-53.

[233] Simon, p. 47; Robert L. Wilson, Letter to WHH, February 10, 1866, *HI,.* p. 204.

[234] Thomas, p. 60.

[235] Simon, pp. 63-64

[235] Thomas, p. 61.

[237] Simon, p. 52.

[238] Robert L. Wilson, Letter to WHH, February 10, 1866, *HI.*, p. 204.

[239] Thomas, p. 64.

[240] Wilson, p. 204.

[241] Thomas, p. 64.

[242] Thomas, p. 64.

CHAPTER TWENTY: Lincoln's Emergence as a Storyteller

[243] J. Rowan to WHH, July 3, 1865, *HI.*, p. 69.

[244] William H. Herndon, "New Salem," *The Lincoln Reader,* ed. by Paul M. Angle (New Brunswick: Rutgers University Press, 1947), p. 39 (Herndon's account written in 1889).

[245] Joseph Gillespie to WHH, Jan. 31, 1866, *HI.*, p. 187.

[246] Abner Y. Ellis to WHH, Jan. 23, 1866, *HI.*, p. 171.

[247] J. M. Ruggles to Ida Tarbell, "First Published Address," *The Life of Abraham Lincoln*, Vol.1, p. 1132: A public domain reprint by BiblioBazaar, LLC.

[248] Abner Y. Ellis Statement to WHH, Dec. 6, 1866, *HI.*, p. 501.

[249] Charles H. Hart to WHH, March 3, 1866, *HI.*, pp. 222-223.

[250] Henry C. Whitney, excerpt from *Life on the Circuit with Lincoln* (Boston: Estes and Lauriat, 1892, pp. 42-49), in *The Lincoln Reader,* p. 169.

[251] "First Debate with Stephen A. Douglas at Ottawa, Illinois, August 21, 1858," Roy Basler, ed., Vol. III., p. 17.

[252] Joshua F. Speed to WHH, Dec. 6. 1866, *HI.,* p. 499.

[253] William H. Herndon to Jesse Weik, Nov.17, 1885, *The Hidden Lincoln,* From the Letters and Papers of William H. Herndon, by Emanuel Hertz (New York: The Viking Press, 1938), p. 104.

CHAPTER TWENTY-ONE: Becoming a Lawyer and Moving to Springfield

[254] David Davis interview by WHH, Sept. 20, 1866, *HI.,* p. 349.

[255] Braden, p. 54.

[256] Braden, p. 55; see also, Donald, pp. 238-241.

INDEX

Adams, John 54
Addison, Joseph Allen, 25
Aesop's Fables,` 23, 24, 97
Allen, John, 73
Arabian Nights, 23
Armstrong, Jack, 66
Arnold, Isaac. 26
Autobiography of Benjamin
 Franklin, 23

Bailey, Nathan, 29
Baldwin, John, 51
Berry, William 69-70
Basler, Roy, 55
Bible, 16-18, 20-21, 22, 23
Bingham, Caleb, 29
"Blab" schools. 20-21
Black HawkWar, 66. 87
Blackstone, William, 66-67
Blair, Hugh, 62, 72
Breckenridge, John, 52
Braden, Waldo, 86
Brommel, Bernard, 7
Brooner, Henry, 22, 50
Brooner, Nancy. 6-7
Brooner, Peter. 7
Burlingame, Michael, 46
Bunyan, Paul, 23

Calhoun, John, 69
Chapman, Augustus, 49
Chapman, Harriet Hanks, 48
Clary Grove gang 66
Clay, Henry, 58, 66
Crawford, Elizabeth, 30, 47, 52, 55,
 80
Crawford, Josiah, 4, 7, 56, 80
Commentaries of English Law,
 66

Constitution of the United
 States, 29

Dawson, John, 87
Davis, David, 97
Davis, Rodney, 55
Day by Day, 66
DeFoe, Daniel, 23
Dilworth, Thomas, 20, 23
Dorsey, Azel, 25-26
Douglas, Stephen, 86, 87, 91,
 97, 100, 101
Duncan, Joseph, 92
Duncan, K. 39

"Elegy Written in a Country
 Courtyard," 62
Ellis, Abner, 39, 86, 88, 96
English Grammar in Familiar
 Lectures, etc., 68
English Reader, 52, 59, 61-62
Euclid, Geometry, 75

Franklin, Benjamin, 23, 58
Farmer, Aaron, 54

Gentry, Allen, 32, 33-34
Gentry, James, 30, 32, 80
Gentry, Matthew, 46
Geometry, 75
Gesell, Arnold, 2, 19, 43
Gillespie, Joseph, 96
Goodwin, Doris Kearns, 7
Graham, Elizabeth, 69
Graham, Jeremiah, 67

Graham, Mentor, 23, 39, 53,
 65, 66-70, 73, 76-77, 80, 84
Graham, Robert, 67

116

ABOUT THE AUTHORS

Vito N. Silvestri, Ph.D. is Professor Emeritus of Communication Studies, Emerson College, and Adjunct Professor of Communication at Florida Gulf Coast University. He is the author of *JFK: A Profile in Communication* (Praeger: 2000), and a textbook, *Interpersonal Communication, 3rd.ed.* (American Press, 1993). He is also the Founder of The Bach Ensemble, Inc. in Naples, Florida.

Alfred P. Lairo has been a lifelong student of Abraham Lincoln and a resident of Sangamon County, Illinois. His interest in Abraham Lincoln was stimulated by living and working in the Sangamon County area most of his life, and this has led him to several years of study about Lincoln as a local figure as well as a national one.

CPSIA information can be obtained at www.ICGtesting.com
Printed in the USA
LVOW13s0359131113

361012LV00003B/5/P